CREATIVITY IN TIMES OF CONSTRAINT

Systemic Thinking and Practice Series

Charlotte Burck and Gwyn Daniel (Series Editors)

This influential series was co-founded in 1989 by series editors David Campbell and Ros Draper to promote innovative applications of systemic theory to psychotherapy, teaching, supervision, and organisational consultation. In 2011, Charlotte Burck and Gwyn Daniel became series editors, and aim to present new theoretical developments and pioneering practice, to make links with other theoretical approaches, and to promote the relevance of systemic theory to contemporary social and psychological questions.

Other titles in the Series include

(For a full listing, see our website www.karnacbooks.com)

The Performance of Practice: Enhancing the Repertoire of Therapy with Children and Families
   Jim Wilson

The Dialogical Therapist: Dialogue in Systemic Practice
   Paolo Bertrando

Systems and Psychoanalysis: Contemporary Integrations in Family Therapy
   Carmel Flaskas and David Pocock

Intimate Warfare: Regarding the Fragility of Family Relations
   Martine Groen and Justine Van Lawick

Being with Older People: A Systemic Approach
   Edited by Glenda Fredman, Eleanor Anderson, and Joshua Stott

Mirrors and Reflections: Processes of Systemic Supervision
   Edited by Charlotte Burck and Gwyn Daniel

Race and Culture: Tools, Techniques and Trainings: A Manual for Professionals
   Reenee Singh and Sumita Dutta

The Vibrant Relationship: A Handbook for Couples and Therapists
   Kirsten Seidenfaden and Piet Draiby

The Vibrant Family: A Handbook for Parents and Professionals
   Kirsten Seidenfaden, Piet Draiby, Susanne Søborg Christensen, and Vibeke Hejgaard

Culture and Reflexivity in Systemic Psychotherapy: Mutual Perspectives
   Edited by Inga-Britt Krause

Positions and Polarities in Contemporary Systemic Practice: The Legacy of David Campbell
   Edited by Charlotte Burck, Sara Barratt, and Ellie Kavner

Creative Positions in Adult Mental Health: Outside In–Inside Out
   Edited by Sue McNab and Karen Partridge

Emotions and the Therapist: A Systemic–Dialogical Approach
   Paolo Bertrando

Surviving and Thriving in Care and Beyond: Personal and Professional Perspectives
   Edited by Sara Barratt and Wendy Lobatto

CREATIVITY IN TIMES OF CONSTRAINT

A Practitioner's Companion in Mental Health and Social Care

Jim Wilson

KARNAC

First published in 2017 by
Karnac Books Ltd
118 Finchley Road, London NW3 5HT

Copyright © 2017 to Jim Wilson.

The right of Jim Wilson to be identified as the author of this work has been asserted in accordance with §§77 and 78 of the Copyright Design and Patents Act 1988.

All rights reserved. No part of this publication may be reproduced, stored in a retrieval system, or transmitted, in any form or by any means, electronic, mechanical, photocopying, recording, or otherwise, without the prior written permission of the publisher.

British Library Cataloguing in Publication Data

A C.I.P. for this book is available from the British Library

ISBN 978 1 78220 201 1

Edited, designed and produced by The Studio Publishing Services Ltd
www.publishingservicesuk.co.uk
email: studio@publishingservicesuk.co.uk

Printed in Great Britain

www.karnacbooks.com

CONTENTS

ACKNOWLEDGEMENTS	vii
ABOUT THE AUTHOR	ix
SERIES EDITORS' FOREWORD	xi
FOREWORD by Imelda McCarthy	xv
PROLOGUE Woolwich Barracks from the bus	xxv
INTRODUCTION	xxvii
CHAPTER ONE Systemic humanism and the ethics of practice	1
CHAPTER TWO Hope, and doing what is possible	15
CHAPTER THREE Exploring creativity in context	37

CHAPTER FOUR
Listening and responding: ethical practices and constraints   59

CHAPTER FIVE
Co-creative supervision and practice: 83
experiment, improvise, and perform

CHAPTER SIX
Forces that push us from behind   115

CHAPTER SEVEN
How do we keep on keeping on?   137

EPILOGUE
The journey home   155

NOTE   157

REFERENCES   159

INDEX   165

ACKNOWLEDGEMENTS

I have been encouraged to "keep on keeping on" in the preparation of this book by my meetings with colleagues from many different practice contexts in many different countries. I wish to give a special thank you to Justine van Lawick, Peter Rober, Rolf Sundet, Ausra Punderva, Rosana Rapizo, Jochen Schweitzer, Vratja Srnad, Rachel Williams, Liz Gregory, and Lars Lungman, all of whom have generously shared their ideas on how to keep creativity alive in their practice and encouraged me to pursue the completion of the book when I was hard pressed with other, more imminent, work commitments.

I wish to mark my appreciation of my colleagues from Greenwich Child and Adolescent Mental Health Service, who were a shining example of how creativity and a generous spirit could be nurtured in the face of much organisational change in an extremely busy service. The members of "Room Five" and the family therapy team deserve special thanks, as do Marcus Averbeck, Teresa Wilson, Adam Goran, and Rekha Vara, whose collegiate friendship and stimulation I valued greatly.

I wish to thank Routledge for giving permission to include certain case vignettes from my contribution to *Narrative Therapies with Children and their Families* (2016).

Glenda Fredman and Jan Parker provided sensitive and robust support in their detailed and rigorous attention to earlier drafts of the text. It was as if they were sitting on either side of me, helping me to stay on track and nudging me when I needed a sharper eye on the direction of travel. Their contributions have been invaluable in deepening my study and clarifying my ideas. Thank you both.

I also thank my friends and associates, Gerry Cunningham, Ian Watson, Sigurd Reimers, and Bengt Weine for our stimulating conversations about the political significance of the topic and its relevance for practitioners and policy makers. The series editors, Gwyn Daniel and Charlotte Burck, together helped me to hold a broad vision for the book, and to highlight areas that needed clearer exposition. Their collegiate support has been very significant in bringing the project to conclusion.

I also wish thank Fi Windsor, artist and teacher, for creating the vibrant watercolour painting for the front cover.

The book would not have been completed had it not also been for the help of Sian, my wife, whose encouragement from first scribble to final word has been unstintingly unselfish. I also thank her for the careful proofreading of the final draft that she carried out with a teacher's scrupulous dedication and the incision of her red pen.

A special acknowledgement goes to John Shotter, my friend and co-presenter at seminars and workshops over the past ten years. John died in December 2016; he is greatly missed by me and by many colleagues touched by his rich contribution to the fields of systemic therapy, consultation, and organisational studies. His constant curiosity about what therapists do helped me to value, all the more, the creative possibilities in our practice. John's enduring passion to explore our social worlds through philosophy and political analysis, together with his career-long critique of academic psychology, has been a constant spur to my thinking. He described himself as a "conversational junkie" and, if so, I was also a happy addict in his company.

What really matters is to try to make our lives as social beings a mutually enriching endeavour with those we meet. John kept this idea alive in his manner of meeting with me and in our joint teaching. He illuminated the intricacy of human connection and an appreciation that every conversation is a new beginning.

ABOUT THE AUTHOR

Jim Wilson is a systemic psychotherapist, working within the National Health Service in Child and Adolescent Mental Health; his career spans practice in social care services and the voluntary and independent sectors. He currently works as a family therapist at Llwyn Onn Child and Family Psychology Service, part of Aneurin Bevan Health CareTrust.

Jim is past chairperson of the Centre for Child Studies at the Institute of Family Therapy, London, and past chair of The Family Institute in Wales.

His publications, which are widely used in training courses in the UK, and in many other countries have been translated into several languages.

He presents his work nationally and internationally and provides consultation, training, and supervision in the UK, mainland Europe, South America, and the Far East.

Jim lives in South Wales, is an enthusiastic guitar player, and is married with four children.

*This book is dedicated to Emily and Finley,
the next generation*

SERIES EDITORS' FOREWORD

Charlotte Burck and Gwyn Daniel

The practice of psychotherapy, whether in private or public domains, has always been inextricably—if at times invisibly—linked to the wider social and political contexts within which it is embedded. These systems and their ideologies reach into the very heart of our professional identities, into the intimate processes of our work with families, shaping our sense of what actions and discourses are available to us and highlighting the contradictions we face between precept and practice, between ethics and pragmatics. There are specific periods in history, however, when political and economic ideologies seem to converge especially starkly with organisational practices that are experienced as oppressive and dehumanising, even though the rhetoric accompanying them often conceals this. These are times when practitioners can feel most powerless and inadequate but when it is especially important to take into account what is happening in the wider political sphere.

In this context, as Jim Wilson argues, practitioners can find themselves trapped into carrying out procedures that seem to bear little resemblance to professional ethics and values, which alienate them from their professional identity and interfere with their connection to their clients. Through this process, individuals can become locked into repeating loops, aware that their activity is pointless, but, nevertheless, feeling unable to resist the practices required of them, no matter how senseless they seem. Connections to fellow practitioners, the bonds of teamwork and opportunities for creative dialogue, can diminish in the face of increasing demands for bureaucratic accounting, form filling, and top-down procedures which bear little relationship to individual circumstances.

Jim Wilson's volume is a powerful counter-blast to the deadening and demoralising effect that procedures of what can be termed "relentless monitoring" can induce in practitioners, leaving them, as he writes, struggling to recognise themselves in the job they do. His contribution is especially welcome at a time of chronic underfunding in mental health services, especially those for children and adolescents, the context that Jim is writing about.

Using the radical humanist framework of Paolo Freire, Jim Wilson expands his vision to put in an eloquent plea for what he calls "systemic humanism". This includes an insistence on searching for social and relational connections in an individualised, diagnosis-led service culture, an argument for maintaining curiosity and uncertainty in a system which creates a drive towards closure, and, above all, a demand for upholding reflexivity, placing the self, the social and cultural hinterland, and the values of the practitioner at the heart of therapeutic practice.

Much of Jim's book, as its title suggests, consists of his argument that supporting the creativity of practitioners and valuing their creative practices is in itself a way of resisting and challenging totalising ideologies which stifle the human spirit. As a practitioners' companion, it is designed to act as an interlocutor, a mentor, or even simply as a friend to those many practitioners who feel demoralised, anxious, and isolated in their work. As many of the case examples demonstrate, Jim is adept at highlighting how quite simple acts of human generosity, kindness, or shared humour can transform relationships and provide a different context from which to face the challenges of the work. His approach is to invite the reader into a sense of feeling that 'we can all do this differently' at the same time as never minimising the effects of power and oppression.

This book will be useful to all those who seek new inspiration in their work. Those who have read Jim's previous volumes (*Child-Focused Practice*, 1998, and *The Performance of Practice*, 2007) will know that he has a wonderful capacity to seek out creative openings in the most stuck or conflictual situations, demonstrating on every page his conviction that by engaging with spontaneity, humility, flexibility, and openness something different will emerge. This approach, as he iterates throughout the book, counteracts the rigidities of systems that are geared towards bureaucratic procedures, rigid manualised treatments, or narrowly defined treatment outcomes.

As ever in Jim's work, there is space for the unexpected, the "left field", the capacity to expand small openings, the seizing of opportunities to transform relationships—all of which he subsumes under the idea of a "possibilist" stance. This is as much a state of mind as it is a method of working and there are many examples in the book of ways that hard-pressed professionals can feel re-energised if their own ideas and resources are activated.

Jim's lively writing style, his humour, his mix of personal and professional narratives, his compelling case examples, his skill at relating complex ideas to the exigencies of everyday challenges and constraints in public services as well as to the idiosyncrasies of individual lives, is what makes this book so compelling and engaging.

This book will be of interest to a very wide range of people working within mental health and social care services, whether or not they are already familiar with systemic ideas. We are delighted to include it in our series.

FOREWORD

Imelda McCarthy

In the opening lines of Jim Wilson's introduction, I am drawn to the words, "we reduce our analysis to individual failings rather than a consideration of the social–relational and political dimensions which largely shape the experience of human distress". These words are followed by the question, "what can we do?" These words, and this question, evoked in me memories of the early days of systemic practice, when that question came from an enthusiastic embracing of different ways to think about clients, problems, and contexts. In those days, an individual orientation held sway, whether it was psychoanalytically, psychodynamically, biologically, or behaviourally orientated. Here, individual failings and pathologies were also the order of the day. However, after the Second World War, it was clear in the mental health professions that many of those presenting with problems were victims of the traumas of war, violence, and fighting. Context became more important in understanding the aetiology of the "complaint". So, the questions "what can we do" and "how can we do it" were filled with excitement, compassion, and hope. The way that practitioners avoided being sanctioned at the time was to learn to be multi-lingual, as it were, and respectful of other approaches by using the appropriate clinical language in different situations. However, this was done alongside a more subversive developing of alliances with other like minds in beginning to experiment with systemic, relational, contextually based practices. For many years, this sub-version was under the radar, so to speak, in the face of the individually orientated hegemony. Then, as with all cycles, they eventually played themselves out, and more options emerged with the flowering of the field of systemic practice.

I love the invitation to such companionship offered by Jim Wilson all through this book. It has been my experience, too, that it is only through companionship and connection that we can once again begin to make a difference that enhances our work. Each of us is called to action, but we cannot do it alone. We need community, we need support, and we need reflective spaces to nurture our selves and our practices. We need this, most of all, to be in service to the wellbeing of others—clients and bureaucrats, managers, and policy makers. What is inspiring here is that there is no call to collapse our field into either/or, them or us camps. Rather, the call is towards the fostering of a kind of quantum field where all co-exist in a cradle where creativity can emerge. The clarion call, "why is this so?", is voiced as a co-creative critical attempt to challenge the recent increasing constrictions and contractions of neo-liberalism and to invite different and diverse perspectives.

Radical systemic humanism

Holding the book together is a coherent ethical, contextual, and compassionate model of thinking and practice wisdom: radical systemic humanism. This orientation comes from the author's early inspiration by the work of Paulo Freire, the Brazilian educationalist who worked to educate the marginalised in relation to the social and political contexts surrounding them. Fellowship and solidarity were embraced over isolation and individualism in the creative educational processes he engaged in (Freire, 1996, p. 66). The kind of critique that systemic humanism allows for can be hidden through the opacity that arises when we are under too much pressure to think and see. Throughout the text, there is a clarion call to see through this opacity and contraction, and open space for a practice based on the wellbeing of all. This call is accompanied by contextual critique and suggested practices, which can help to throw open the windows and allow the fresh air of creative responses to flow through again. As Wilson states, it allows breathing space for reflection and a new enthusiasm based on our core values to become visible once more. Then we see something new or, even more relevantly, try something new. "We allow for creative risk taking" especially when "we feel that our abilities and experiences are recognised and validated by others. We are invited into creativity, and the challenge is in how we might respond". This is the constant invitation made to the readers of this book.

Policies hiding oppressive practices?

Under the guise of efficiency and savings, slick discourses emerged, turning clients into customers and agencies into macro- and mini-businesses where services were purchased and provided. It all seemed so smooth until we realised that it hid cost cutting that inflated profits for the private bodies now in the place of providing the purchased services. More and more the interests of services users took a back seat and the morale and possibilities of those employed and commissioned to serve them descended into contraction, box ticking, manualisation, and "must do" directions. This book inserts itself into this context and stands for an archaeology of hope and resilience, curiosity, aliveness, creativity, and a relational ethics. There is no moral hubris intended here, just the illumination of a critical and systemic curiosity with regard to relational realities rather than number crunching and pathology ratings.

It seems to me that the author is pointing the way beyond restrictive and deterministic practices of individual or biomedical focii towards the open vistas and the full spectrum of the richness and potential of human experience. It is a possibility frame rather than a prejudicial frame. Like Freire, Wilson offers us, the readers, a framework that is conscientised in relation to social, political, and economic orders that distort the landscape of human possibilities. Curiosity, companionship, or what he refers to as mutual humanisation and learning, then becomes a kind of gentle, yet powerful, dissent, protest, and subversion. This has echoes of Nora Bateson's beckonings towards what she calls "symmathesy" (mutual learning) in trans-contextual milieux (Bateson, 2016). Workers and clients are no longer shrunken into singular prescriptions or descriptions of reduced functioning and possibilities, through restrictive evidence-based practices on the one hand, and pathologising, individualising labels on the other hand.

Nowhere in this textual work are we far from a practice that combines a rigorous analysis of context and one's own personal predilections as a therapist. There is a constant engagement in a reflexive curiosity between self and context in the avoidance of a top-down, regulated treatment regime bound by evidences often not relevant to clients' lives. Digging our heels in is not an option in Wilson's world. Rather, an openness to diversity and possibility is everywhere imagined and explored. In this, we can hear the voice of that genius of clinical thinking and practice, Gianfranco Cecchin, as he invites us to curiosity and irreverence and away from those romantic involvements, that "falling in love" with prejudices and fixed ideas (Cecchin et al., 1992). Such relational orientations evoke an embrace of uncertainty. There can never be certainty in the swampy terrain of constant recalibrations and responsivity in the "to-ing" and "fro-ing" of experiential sharing of contextually hued, lived experiences. Humility and awe are the recommended antidotes to professional hubris and imagined certainty. Certainty has no sure foothold in situations where identities need space to move in response to different contextual necessities they encounter.

We have many identity expressions or, indeed, identities that are called forth by the different relationships in our lives: mother–father, daughter–son, child–adult, teacher–student, professional–client, expert, and so on. Similar identities arise in relation to gender, race, religion, ability, class, ethnicity, education . . . When we have a mingling of these identities among professionals and clients or client systems, there is a complexity that can never be reduced to a tick-box mentality or any kind of certainty. Instead, there is an ongoing dance of difference, diversity, and possibilities. Versatility and spontaneity, not singularity and prescription, are what is needed in the development of "repertoires of creativity" (Wilson, 2007).

This is the proposed art of therapy, which is not in opposition to a science of therapy. However, each is situationally or contextually coherent and resonant. Hence, the need and call for an ongoing critical self-reflexivity in relation to contexts of social and economic contraction, deprivation, injustice, and impoverishment. Otherwise, there is the spectre of probability that, without companionship and self-reflexivity, we will fall prey to invitations to pathologise, demonise, and blame those clients who are unable to fit with the proscribed ways of living and dong things. Contextual awareness, thus, broadens our lens and discourse beyond "just self–other awareness". Compassion and love shines through in this text, as we are reminded again and again of the interfacing of our personal experiences and those of our clients in situations of hope and desperation.

Order out of chaos?

So, how does one balance the realities of today's practitioner worlds with hope? How do we combine dissidence with pragmatics? After all, the intention is not to get fired unless as a last resort, I would imagine. However, for those who have the daily frustrations of living with the constraints on and of the current service institutions, this is no easy matter. What do we do with our frustrations and anger when we see children offered drugs when their main issues are more relevantly associated with the particular relational and social contexts in which their lives are embedded? Wilson, thus, asks the very pertinent questions, "how can we effectively speak out and up, not lose heart while not succumbing to false hopes?" A tall order, one might say, in today's world, and yet that is precisely both our challenge and invitation. How do we, through companionship, systemic analysis, and a humanising orientation nurture our (co-)creativity? Such questions are not only questions of how we serve our clients in the best way, but also how we safeguard our own wellbeing as professionals in today's world. Isolation is hardly the way. We need our like-minded companions. Along with companions, Wilson also pairs hope and hopelessness as possible twin harbingers of a call to new creative situations provided we do not overfeed both. Over-identifying with hopelessness leads to tiredness, a lack of energy, and a kind of pessimism that can deter us from finding possibilities. I am reminded here of the physicist Ilya Prigogine and his Nobel awarded theory of "Order out of chaos" (Prigogine & Stengers, 1984). Sometimes, we need the impetus of chaos to shake us out of our "business as usual", out of our habituated boxes, to generate new creativities for our selves and others.

If we think in a first order systemic way (which is often helpful), then there is always an end to the downwards spiral, at which systems tend once again to recalibrate towards a rebalancing, frequently at a higher level of operation. In these situations, imagination is another wonderful companion. Imagining futures, which are different to difficult presents, has long been a soothsayer for those in challenging situations. This is a kind of letting the light in through the cracks, as Leonard Cohen might have said. So, challenging times bring with them many cracks when we have the eyes to see them. Our choice, then, is the old one. Can we see the light through the cracks? Are we part of the problem or part of the solution? This book, for me, reminds us that we can be both. Practising with a non-contextual awareness, we become part of the problem, but when we open up our awareness to the contextual plays surrounding us all, then we can avoid the pitfalls associated with our part in problem generating and embrace possibilities of generating new dialogical realities. Crises can become "turning points". We all become interacting subjects in the contextual play, and not objects of scrutiny and labelling.

Fun, respect, and creativity in the face of the colonisation of contextual practices

Reading through this book, I am again and again delighted by the creativity, analysis, humour, compassion, and practical turn of the author. We are taken with both broad and slender brushstrokes into the heart of the labyrinth of each client–family dilemma, while simultaneously being offered Ariadne's thread as a metaphoric way forward. Knowing Jim Wilson, one is also aware of his talent for improvisation and creativity as he gently and often humorously walks his talk. His summations at the end of each chapter are those steps we can consider to take us out of our own specific boxes, dilemmas, or, maybe, even fear at this time. The gentleness and clarity of these summations, however, also invite us to share a glimpse of a more expanded vista of possibility, open social mindedness, and even good playful fun.

Contextual knowledge, wisdom, and "grace" enter this text as a fully embodied responsiveness combined with an open space theoretical appreciation. Techniques offered in an open-minded and open-hearted way are no longer discredited as manipulative or outdated. Here, all the jewels of systemic work are placed at the feet of clients and services, as it were. Nothing is discarded except disregard for the music of those seeking "help". Wilson returns again and again through this text to the concept of irreverence. We can become irreverent of our prejudices and also see it as a political act and a way of picking up possibilities for "challenging old ways of thinking and doing". Importantly, Wilson reminds us that "whistleblowing" can also be a form of necessary irreverence when what we observe is experienced as counter to the wellbeing of clients and good practices.

We are provoked, in reading this text, to examine many of the pernicious feedback loops that can impinge upon, or constitute, our practice in times of form-filling and ticking boxes. In complying, being reverent, we co-create a potential illusion of keeping our jobs and our salaries, but at what cost? What of wellbeing and ethical living and working? In times of shrinking services, we might not keep our jobs and we might also have sold ourselves out in the process. This is a welcome jolt to our reverence for the status quo and competing professional excellences. Open, collaborative teamwork has a hard time to survive in such a context. But it is nothing short of life saving to make sure it does. For me, there is a particularly glowing moment of creative team dissidence when a staff team posted a cartoon lampooning current orthodoxies on the side of a filing cabinet for the staff, but not the bosses, to see. In this act of resistance, I am reminded of that colonial subversion when a poor man bent low and farted as the king passed by. We should not forget that, although it might look otherwise, colonised communities find ways to use humour, poetry, music, and the arts to both resist and to survive.

Wilson is never afraid to distinguish between what he refers to as anaesthetic and aesthetic practices, and, in many places throughout the text, we see him as a playmate practitioner, as it were. He gets down on the floor with children, improvises, and role-plays with clients of all ages. This kind of performance is taken into both consultation and supervision, when therapists are asked to role-play a family's dilemma while the family becomes a reflecting team. Old, one-way linearities and singular descriptions have, thus, a chance to fall away or fall into each other in the creation of a more diverse landscape of thinking and acting. Supervision is viewed in its complexity and context. Here, Wilson is bringing his decades of experience to bear in different kinds of institutions with different kinds of mandates. Contextual sensitivity is never lost when therapists are caught between the rock and the hard place that is an individual and evidence-based linearity and constantly contracting budgets and resources. It can be a little like that scene in *Alice in Wonderland* when she is lost in the forest and exposed to a multiplicity of conflicting signposts: diverse identities, and medical opinions, complexity and linearity, uncertainty and certainty, individualism and systemics. Placed alongside each other in a both/and frame, relationality is no longer in danger of being lost in Wilson's performative practices in supervision and therapy. A stance of self-reflective humility and humour is ever present to lighten potential ways forward. Nowhere is a magician therapist imagined, but, rather, the magic of a relational and contextual aesthetic.

Throughout, the breadth of Jim Wilson's practice history is in evidence. He has worked in statutory, voluntary, and private sectors as a social worker and systemic humanist practitioner. He is a therapist, supervisor, consultant, and, I would say, coach. This has all provided him with a diverse experience and viewpoints from which to survey the current landscape of cut-backs, regulation, evidence-based practices, manuals, and tick sheets of "must dos". Interestingly, he also sees himself contributing from the sidelines in opening up exploratory dialogues and reflection spaces for observing current, everyday practices. Across these islands in the North Atlantic, we have a tradition of manuscripts from the eighth to the tenth centuries where many of the important illuminations are in the margins. Here, in this text, we have countless "marginal illuminations" (McCarthy & Byrne, 2008).

In this text, Wilson, always cognisant of his systemic and contextual positioning, offers a way through the maze of increasingly difficult, staff demoralising, and non-client centred services orientations. This book is his attempt to help therapists to keep going on through co-creating dialogues so that we can avoid being monologically positioned and losing faith in what we know to be "better" practices for our clients, ourselves, and our agencies. However, the focus for such co-creation also extends to political movements aimed at addressing the direction of neo-liberal policies and practices.

Systemic humanist dissidence and the neo-liberal agenda

I think all of us in practice have experienced what Wilson refers to as forces behind our backs pushing us in certain directions. Sometimes, there is so much pressure that we just get on with the tasks in hand and pay as little attention as we can to the background "noise", as it were. This background noise can be greater bureacratisation, privatisation, models, manuals and measurements, surveillance and regulation, social disconnection, and dehumanisation. In today's world of social and mental health care, these headlines have become the dominant discourses in many of our major service providers. However, as Jim Wilson reminds us, when we remain aware of our contexts, this can be the first step to altering them by asking pertinent systemic questions. I love Wilson's likening of manuals to musical scores when they help cue us towards some helpful markers and ideas. However, the magic happens when relationality, or *human*isation is included to bring it to life.

So, are we part of the problem or part of the solution? When we become passive, we can become "domesticated" and so constitute the very conditions that are damaging our clients and ourselves. We need those dreams, songs, poems, and art to support aliveness and wellbeing. How can we "build a city to live in", as Irish author James Stephens asked in *A Crock of Gold*, his fairy tale for adults and children alike. It is not just about us as therapists, it is about building a whole human society that is relationally based, where we help our neighbours and "strangers" alike, where we do not cast blame upon people for their vulnerabilities. What happens to one happens to all is very well illustrated in the work of the Equality Trust in the UK (2016). More equal societies shower wellbeing across all social classes. More unequal societies do the opposite, even in the lives of the so-called well off. So, we need to be constantly on guard so that the four "M's" (monetarism, manualisation, marketisation, and marginalisation) can be transformed into the four "C's" (care, consistency, conscientiousness, and commitment).

Last, and most importantly, this book is offered as a textual companion to support readers in their journeys as co-creative, compassionate, conscientious social actors, and, indeed, activists in the interests of serving well, relationally, resourcefully, honestly, and in solidarity with our clients, our colleagues (micro politics). In this way, perhaps, the current process of dehumanisation in our social and health care services can change (macro politics). "Must dos" need to be placed in the service of those we are commissioned to serve and not the market-led commissioners in their bottom-line practices and policies.

In closing, Wilson honours all those colleagues who have co-created a "home" with him in fostering atmospheres of professional belongingness. I, too, in my career, must say that it was the single most important thing in fostering my ongoing passion for our field. I refuse to give up.

PROLOGUE

Woolwich Barracks from the bus

The young recruits are in full military uniform with rucksacks which, going by the strained expressions on their faces, are fully loaded with all that is required to do battle. The soldiers jog up the hill alongside the bus in which I am travelling to work at the Mental Health Service, Greenwich. I am daydreaming; I look at the determination on the faces of these recruits. No one wants to be left behind. They need to prove their worth, their strength and willingness to engage in combat, whatever forms that might take. I think about my colleagues and the increasing workload, waiting lists, "must dos", and the next "top-down" directive to administer.

What happens to us when anxiety takes a firm hold and threatens compassion, companionship, and mutual support? We carry an increasingly heavy caseload, but why such a weight? These days, each practitioner is loaded with additional performance standards, procedural and bureaucratic duties, and weighty feelings of scrutiny that make the load even heavier, despite the claim that such steps are designed for greater efficiency and effectiveness. The practitioner in mental health and social care is out of breath, frightened to be perceived as a straggler, and worried that if they do not manage to keep up they will not be fit for purpose. But what purpose?

The bus nears the hospital. I can feel tightness in my neck muscles and slight tension in my stomach. I recollect a colleague who said recently that the most important question for a practitioner to ask of himself is, "Do I recognise myself in the job that I do?" This question sits with me as I enter the hospital for the start of the day.

INTRODUCTION

> "Our life is part folly, part wisdom. Whoever writes about it only reverently and according to the rules leaves out more than half of it"
>
> (de Montaigne, 2004)

The passion for writing this book comes from a deep and lasting dissatisfaction with the way clients and practitioners must accommodate procedures for working together which reduce complex social and psychosocial problems to single pathways for treatment, often leading to dead ends. When practitioners are caught in the same reductive analysis, wider contextual features become invisible. The practitioner is considered "not up to the job" rather than the job becoming an increasingly impossible task to perform within one's capabilities. We reduce our analysis to individual failings rather than a consideration of the social–relational and political dimensions which largely shape the experience of human distress.

"What can we do?" I hear the disillusioned practitioner ask. "We have to put up with these changes in procedures to keep our jobs!"

This is a very important point. It is natural when we feel threatened to huddle together for protection and comfort. Tight financial budgets and reorganisational strategies to "refresh" or rationalise services create anxiety about job security in which perceived threats of competition from other similarly constrained disciplines can lead to divisiveness and mistrust. When there is less food on the table, it is tempting to snatch rather than share.

The demise of creative partnerships between colleagues is a disaster for the clients and for the services that are intended to provide help. The thrust of my argument in this book is to preserve, sustain, and enrich practice with a commitment to solidarity and companionship between practitioners from whichever discipline. Mental health and social care services are inevitably shaped by wider socio–political forces. These forces are implemented through policies and procedures that directly affect the way treatments are provided. But, where problems are reduced to individual failings, deficits, and pathologies, it is easy to see why the wider social features of practice can be marginalised.

The desire to continue to practise with creativity and imagination is what keeps many practitioners going. In discussions with colleagues from many different settings and cultural contexts, I routinely hear that what keeps inspiration alive is the satisfaction found in direct face-to-face contact with clients, together with creative processes of support and supervision. We need each other to debate and take whatever action is possible to preserve this crucial weave of partnership between practitioners and our clients.

This book is an invitation to companionship; to reflect on what it is possible to do to counter such constraints and remain true to the values and ideals that brought you into the job you do. Without critical reflection, we can become docile, but without action to do what is possible, we become resigned to accept that which offends our professional values and stifles creativity.

Within these pages, I hope you will find inspiration to sustain and nourish your own practice. Creativity is placed here as a context of co-construction. It does not reside as a "magical" component of the exceptionally creative therapist. Here, I emphasise the social and relational features that can inspire or constrain each of us. Of course, there is no clear divide between constraints and creative practices. Limitations can inspire innovation that later might become a constraint. Think of those times when a new technique has been employed by you with good effect only later to become a redundant aspect of your repertoire. We hone ideas and techniques from our experience as practitioners, and make them into something that constitutes our ways of working—our "style". This is unique and is always open to development if we choose to remain curious about what we try to do to improve our effectiveness. I have used the term, "practitioner's companion", because I hope to exemplify creative practices alongside the concerns expressed to me by colleagues in many different settings and countries where services are under threat. I place myself squarely in the picture as I explore my doubts and aspirations to "recognise myself in the job I do". I extend my hand to you to explore these themes for yourself, and talk with others to keep the dialogue open between all of us involved in pushing for effective practice.

Good companions rely on conversation and curiosity to question each other's assumptions. Creative possibilities already exist in our practice, and can be enhanced by challenging assumptions about how we should proceed. In asking, "Why is this so?" we celebrate difference and encourage debate. The teacher, mental health practitioner, and social work colleague are all trained to exercise curiosity and critical capacities in their practice. We are trained to be able to entertain many possibilities in order to assist our clients. It follows, then, that our job is *also* to focus on the constraints that feature within our own disciplines and organisations, otherwise we consider only one side of our relationship to practice.

It is the *processes* of creativity and constraint that I wish to address in all their complexity. Service managers face constraints, commissioners face restrictions; the team leaders, head teachers, and social care managers I meet regularly discuss the effects of constraints upon them, whether financial, bureaucratic, or policy driven. I also wish to avoid the trap of dividing *us* (the creative practitioners) from *them* (the cold-hearted bureaucrats); rather, I emphasise both the conditions that are detrimental to effective practice and those that instil a creative drive towards good service delivery for all involved, practitioners, managers, policy makers, and, especially, the clients.

The contextual constraints and circumstances that threaten creativity are threaded through the chapters that follow, and are given specific attention in Chapter Six. I have chosen to do this to avoid any tendency to get lost in the Slough of Despond, which would risk putting out the fire before it has hardly sparked into life. It is akin to those times when we meet clients saturated with talk of problems where no life is left to see the light of their resources and creative possibilities. However, if you are determined to dig straight away into an exploration of the various degrees of constraint, then please go directly to Chapter Six—maybe it will help fire your creativity even more.

Questions that play constantly on my mind, and on the minds of many of my colleagues, are to do with how we can keep going with a generous spirit and a critically reflective attitude. We live with a sense that there is more to appreciate, and more to strive for. In discussion with John Shotter (2016) he quotes the late Tom Andersen (1990), who was constantly aware of a "restlessness that would not leave him alone". These themes are also threaded together in the chapters that follow, with practical illustrations of both the constraints and creative possibilities open to us.

While making an impassioned call for upholding creativity in practice, I have tried to avoid preaching a new list of systemic humanising "must dos"; the invitation is, rather, to explore, discuss, and act ethically in ways that do justice to our professional endeavours to help clients in distress, using whatever means possible, in whatever setting you are practising.

In search of inspiration and companionship

I attend a lecture given by the writer, feminist, and political activist, Nawal El Saadawi. This octogenarian is helped to her seat by a young assistant, and the interviewer begins to ask her questions about her life. I am in the audience, notepad in hand. I have heard about her, and have come to the lecture because I am intrigued to find out what keeps her going against the odds. She was brought up in a poor Egyptian village, did well in school, and became a psychiatrist and, later, a writer and activist against gender and class repression in Egyptian society. She was jailed for her outspoken views against female genital mutilation.

Her responses to the interviewer's questions are taken seriously, with touches of humour and irony. She seems able to take herself seriously but without arrogance, or bitterness towards those who treated her badly in her life. Her irreverent attitude makes me smile.

When asked about what motivates her to speak out despite the risks to her safety she comments (and I paraphrase only slightly),

Creativity is challenge—a sense that something is not right leads us to creativity, to challenge, to resist and to ask the question, why this is so? We learn by questioning. How can we believe in something without questioning it? We get organised by a fear of offending the status quo. Creativity includes acts of dissidence. (Personal communication, October 2015, Bristol Festival of Ideas)

This book finds inspiration in asking ourselves, "Why is this so?" If, instead, we stifle debate for the sake of compliance, we lose the capacity to challenge. When we are not able to challenge, we lose opportunities of a change for the better. The question I pose is how to do this with integrity, with an eye on how to do so in ways that will help all of us to recognise ourselves in the jobs we do and, I would add, in the lives we lead.

Systemic humanism

I have drawn inspiration from Freire's definition of radical humanism (1996) to illuminate my systemic therapy training and my orientation to practice; these combined and ethically affiliated perspectives are encapsulated in the term "systemic humanism".

The principles for systemic humanism, as set out in Chapter One, are intended as guides to keep us alert to the many social and political forces and interests that have a bearing on what we try to do to provide an effective service. I will move between the more distal organisational and political contexts of practice, and the proximal face-to-face interactions with clients. These levels of context are not mutually exclusive; rather, they inform and are informed by one another. Systemic humanist practices such as Freire's radical humanist education are centrally concerned with

> The pursuit of full humanity [that] cannot be carried out in isolation or individualism, but only in fellowship and solidarity; therefore, it cannot unfold in antagonistic relations between oppressor and oppressed. No one can be authentically human while he prevents others from being so. (Freire, 1996, p. 66)

I have aimed to write, as far as possible, in general language, referring to theories and philosophical influences where relevant, but with a deep appreciation of the history of the ideas shaping systemic family therapy approaches over the years. In all the practice illustrations that follow, I have altered any identifying characteristics but have remained as accurate as possible in my recollection of process and narratives described.

Ideals and possibilities

I am presenting a workshop in the UK on the topic of this book, and ask participants to engage in an exercise that explores the limitations to, and possibilities for, the expression of their creativity. (The detail of this exercise is outlined in Chapter Three.)

The buzz that ensues is lively and very vociferous. Participants remark how useful and supportive it is to talk openly with others about the restrictions to their practice and the pressures they must endure, but, more importantly, the discussion leads to focusing on the values that brought them into their profession in the first place. They begin to explore how to challenge constraints to their creativity within their settings, at the same time being thoughtful about what might be possible to do rather than setting up utopian dreams. I am inspired by witnessing their hunger, not only to survive, but also to reinvigorate practice and reach for continued development. At the same time, however, I also feel sad that such conversations have been starved from debate hitherto and elsewhere. First, we must bring matters to light before we can see which direction to take. Doing what is possible to criticise current practice also allows us to remain loyal to our ideals.

> The mere fact that we recognise the importance of ideals that are better than our existing practice does not in itself mean that we are hypocrites. ... It is normal. The whole point of having ideals at all is to criticise current practice. ... If there were a society whose ideals were no more than a description of its existing behaviour it would be almost inconceivably inert. (Midgley, 2001, p. 166)

I intend to leave breathing space at various points in the text to allow for reflection via some questions posed, and exercises on offer, to you. It is the exploration of these questions that can help us to be active in the decisions we take. Yet, like the impossibility of the instruction to "be spontaneous!", there can be no prescriptions on how to "be creative": that is up to each of us in collaboration with those with whom we work, and the clients we meet. At the same time, however, it is both possible and desirable to explore the conditions that promote co-creativity. Creativity through collaboration with others requires sensitivity in knowing when and how to begin to introduce some fresh ideas and activity. This is mutually enriching. The practitioner must sense when the time is right to take a new step, and risk the uncertainty that comes when a novel experience is on the cusp of happening.

I play the guitar, and recently I was invited to sit in with other musicians who had played together as a group for many years. The band allowed me to join them but I was the "new kid on the block", so I had to make sure I did not put myself forward in too pushy a manner. At the same time, I had to show I could measure up, so sitting back too much would also be a mistake. Instead, I waited to hear what others were playing, and tried to add something to what was already being played. I had to accompany the others first. At a particular moment, the group leader gave me the "nod", inviting me to take a solo, which I did with relish. Later, I pondered on the sequence and wondered what had led the group leader to give me the signal to take a solo when he did. Fortunately, I met him again sometime later and asked him if he could recall and comment on what allowed him to give me the nod when he did. He said, "I listen to what everyone is doing and when I listen I can hear what could work [to benefit the music]. So, then I gave you the nod." His reaction is not the atomised separating out of the individual musicians into their specific contributions but, rather, a response to what the music needed at that moment. The "nod" is what we wait for from our clients. It is what the context seems to call for, not what we demand of the other.

When we try something new, we allow for creative risk taking; this is more likely to be done when we feel that our abilities and experiences are recognised and validated by others. We are invited into creativity, and the challenge is in how we might respond. This is the invitation I make to you in the following pages.

CHAPTER ONE

Systemic humanism and the ethics of practice

The term systemic humanism was coined by me to combine key concepts from systemic family therapy with inspiration drawn from the work of Paulo Freire to shape practice more distinctly as a process of humanisation (Wilson, 2015). "Radical humanism" within systemic practice struck me as a necessary emphasis to counteract dehumanising traits that thwart both practitioner and client in the search for creative possibilities to enrich practice.

Systemic humanism emphasises that a practice be both cognisant of, and actively involved in, opposing oppressive practice. It is rooted in ways of enabling our clients and ourselves to become more active, powerful, and creative within the helping process. It explores ways that practitioners, from whichever profession, can remain curious, creative, and alive to possibilities. This involves a consideration of the values that we enact in the jobs we try to do. Practical applications of systemic practice are enriched by reference to Freire's concept of radical humanism in his philosophy of education, which I have found invaluable in my work as a family therapist.

The distinctive features outlined here are intended to encourage practitioners to look wider than the clinical room for inspiration, and to engage in critical analysis of the contexts of practice. I hope that practitioners from different theoretical orientations will take from the following ideas and practices what suits their passion and concerns. Systemic humanism is a call to think and practise with a critical curiosity that crosses disciplinary divides and theoretical stances. We cannot escape ideology, so it is best to have an ideology that is rooted in values of humanism and that is also wise to the political realities that inform, and partially form, who we are.

I include these features at the outset in order that we have shared reference points and a common language to accompany later explorations in the territory of practice. The more we restrict the language of practice to categories, such as individual diagnoses, the more we limit what we see and how we think. I have noticed that, from time to time, I can become drawn into shorthand descriptions of clients' situations, finding myself caught up in categorising typologies of problems for statistical analysis. This might be seen as necessary procedurally, particularly when there is a "tariff" system operating to decide who should gain access to a service under pressure. However, a problem arises when this tendency becomes exaggerated in times of heavy workload pressures, where the effect on practitioners is to begin to think in terms of client numbers rather than the unique circumstances of each client or family. We can, inadvertently, become number crunchers. Practitioners in mental health and social care are not exempt from the processes that promote an ideology that restricts descriptions of clients to categories of dysfunction. Freire claims that, "teachers cannot be effective when they remain in the thrall of an exploitative school system that robs them of their voice" (1998, p. 13). Could the same not be said of practitioners who feel similarly restricted in voicing alternatives to reductive codes of practice? A conscious effort is required to place the social relational and political analysis of a client's predicament centre stage in discussion. The conceptual landmarks set out here place a systemic humanising process in contrast to other perspectives that are focused more keenly on individual or biomedical diagnosis. These more objective formulations fail to take account of the practitioner's own prejudices in seeing what he sees, or thinks he sees. These themes are taken up later when we consider the potential, and actual, limitations placed on practitioners' vision of therapeutic possibilities.

Systemic humanism: principles for ethical practice

All interaction is aimed towards us becoming more fully human

To be more human, in Freire's terms, is to be against ideological determinism, particularly forms of ideology that objectify the other. He stands against fatalism and hopelessness to alter our living conditions. Instead, he calls for an ethic of freedom (not in the neo-liberal sense) that depends on each person's development of a critical curiosity as a necessary feature of one's presence in the world (not just "being") to transform both one's social self and the social contexts of one's life. Freire holds that a humanised society requires cultural freedom, the ability of the individual to choose values and rules of conduct that violate conventional, social norms. However, people cannot raise themselves to bid for power unless their curiosity has been aroused to ask the hard questions: "Why?" as well as "What?" For Freire, then, "the foundation stone of the whole [educational process] is human curiosity. This is what makes me question, know, act, ask again, recognise" (1998, p. 19).

While we are, to a degree, conditioned by our history, we are not determined by it. Freire offers a framework that puts practice squarely within a political and ethical context. His concept of *conscientizacao*, translated into English as critical consciousness, refers to our learning to perceive social, political, and economic conditions that have an impact on, and shape, self-oppressive ways of thinking and being. The process of raising our critical consciousness brings these dimensions of life into focus and promotes action against oppressive elements of our reality. Systemic humanism is both cognisant of, and actively involved in, opposing oppressive practices. This orientation offers a wider landscape of possibilities to us as practitioners, and to those who seek our help, to look within and beyond the clinical setting into the communities and political spheres of influence that have a powerful bearing upon social and mental health problems in our daily practice. Systemic humanist practices are a democratic endeavour emphasising partnership between client/patient/student and practitioner. We are involved in a process of mutual humanisation, and are open to learn from each other. As practitioners, we can feel pushed from behind to comply with values or activities we might not agree with and, at the same time, pulled from the front to remain loyal to humanising values that stir our conscience and direct our practice. This is an ethical tension practitioners often feel caught within, and is expressed in our embodied and intellectual responses to those we meet.

Humility, uncertainty, and mutual learning are interconnected

Practice, as with all interactions between persons, takes place in a context that is multi-sensorial and multi-storied. These ideas stop us in our tracks from being overly convinced that our thoughts and feelings represent the only true picture of a situation. The systemic bias considers that our thoughts and feelings are also dependent on the relational process in which we are currently involved. Our responses are considered as information about what may be occurring in the interaction between us and should be valued, not as a search for absolute truth but, as a direction for possible exploration with the client, or in our personal reflections (Cecchin et al., 1994). For example, if, as a therapist, I feel very drawn to support a child who is vulnerable and unhappy, this response could also be information about what is not happening elsewhere in his life. Of course, my response needs to be critically appraised, because it is also possible that the child "triggers" a reaction in me that might be more to do with my own childhood memories than his lived experience. A systemically informed, reflexive process places my responses as a feature of the current context while also taking account of my own personal biases or prejudices. In this scenario, I might wish to explore more about who else cares for the child, where he feels most "at home" with others, and in what ways he shows that he might need support and emotional containment, and so on.

The idea that there are many possible responses to what we experience allows us to value doubt and encourage curiosity. When I notice myself, "falling in love" with an idea, I try to permit doubt to arise so that I can revise my prejudice. I also need to ask the question "Is this a useful idea to help my practice with this client?" rather than "Is this the true definition or explanation of what is really happening?" If I should become too certain of my opinion, I am more likely to try to convince the other person of the veracity of my version of the truth. Instead, I need to pause to consider other possible views. I may still decide to follow my "hunch" based on further exploration but I cannot afford to close off other opinions, whether contradictory or mutually supportive. Problems arise when our opinions are challenged and it feels like a personal attack. In such a case, I am tempted to dig in my heels, but then, opportunity for useful dialogue is lost. The key idea for practice is to appreciate that the position taken up by each participant will have its own logic and rationale for that person, no matter how strange this might seem to us. Our job is to try to appreciate the rationale and motivation of the other person's point of view first, and in such a way that any enquiry is made from a position of curiosity about the other's view, rather than as an attack upon the individual as a person.

This is an acknowledgement by us that we are in the sway of relatedness, not able to know for sure any outcome:

> Understanding does not reach out and take hold of language; it is carried out within language . . . the hermeneutic process involves not only the moments of understanding and of interpretation but also the moment of application, that is to say, understanding oneself is a part of the process. (Gadamer, cited in Palmer, 2001, p. 37)

Unpredictability is the order of the day, not certainty in what will occur even when we have a definite protocol to follow.

Humility is embedded in humanising practices and stops us from taking ourselves too seriously. Instead, systemic humanism celebrates uncertainty and exploration of alternatives, where opposing viewpoints are welcomed. It allows for the rough edges of certainty and predictability to be rounded off by becoming aware that in meeting with another we cannot know for sure how we may influence or be influenced in the exchange. To try to understand another person better,

> . . . we must take the encounter with the other person seriously, because there is always something about which we are not correct, and are not justified in maintaining. Through an encounter with the other we are lifted above the narrow confines of our knowledge. A new horizon is disclosed that opens onto what was unknown to us. (Gadamer, cited in Palmer, 2001, p. 49)

When power and status back up opinions that run counter to our own views, an additional challenge is to find a way to speak up rather than be cowed by the power of the other to silence dissent. I recall a case conference in which over twenty colleagues were in attendance when I presented a case dilemma for discussion. While everyone listened to the description of my concerns, only the head nurse and psychiatrist contributed their suggestions. When I noticed this, I invited others into the exchange; eventually some nurses and social workers joined in but my invitation for others to speak up was clearly a transgression from the usual form of case discussion in this team. In this instance, the case conference was an enactment of the hierarchical distribution of power within the team, rather than a dialogue about how to make best use of the perspectives of all participants. Professional status trumped the idea of generative dialogue between all participants.

Identities are context dependent

I assume that how we see ourselves is, in part, formed by our cultural histories, and performed and altered through our lived experience in the here and now. To paraphrase the poet, Robert Burns, we cannot see ourselves as others see us but we can critically appraise the way we are seen by others through their responses to us. Identities are always on the move, revised and/or confirmed in interaction, and expressed through all communicative behaviour with others. The signatures of our identities are inscribed in how we enact our professional practices. As human beings, we have many "identities": husband, father, son, brother, Muslim, mother, lover, and so on. Personal resonances might come to mind when we meet with our clients and we might try to find appropriate expressions of our repertoire of identities called upon for making a useful connection as a practitioner. Of course, our clients are doing the same thing, and each meeting is, in fact, a form of improvisation, seeing what fits in our exchanges, and what is not yet ready to be expressed but can be noticed between us. For example, sometimes when I meet with certain clients, I find myself using more informal language and more expansive gestures that remind me of how I might talk with someone from my own working-class background. The point is that these aspects of my cultural and class identity are evoked by the presence, manner, class, or cultural cues presented by the others as I notice their response to my responses, and so on. It does not mean that we are acting falsely; rather, it is recognition of our adaptability and endeavour to connect with the other person through degrees of similarity and difference between us. It is the tension between sameness and difference that can be useful in helping clients to become other than they are, and, in so doing, the practitioner is also affected by such changes in interaction. We learn to see each other differently.

As clients begin to assume more responsibility for changes in their lives, I likewise learn to alter my responses to them, perhaps becoming much less active, following the changes they are instigating rather than provoking new areas for discussion and challenge. We do, indeed, learn from our clients, and this learning can become a storehouse of associations, experiences, and anecdotes that can be brought into play in other situations when called for. I recall one man who had the courage to speak of his childhood abuse to me during the third session of family therapy. Later, when the therapy was coming to an end, he confided that he had decided he could trust me enough with the painful matters of his past because he felt there was sufficient similarity in our ways of talking that made him feel at ease. It is noteworthy that one reason why clients drop out of therapy is when the perceived difference between the client's class and culture and that of the practitioner is too great. Hence, versatility in the performance of our practice will allow us—clients and practitioners—to develop our repertoires of creativity (Wilson, 2007).

Our work is always a meeting between us as human beings, who are also political beings

> Our work is always a meeting point between us as persons, not between us as an experiment. The subject for study is intercommunication between me and the patient meeting on equal terms, each teaching the other, and getting enriched by the experience of involvement. What we do in our work is to arrange a professional setting made up of time and space and behaviour . . . and we see what happens. This is the same as form in art . . . which allows of spontaneous impulse and the unexpected creative gesture. This is what we wait for and value highly in our work, and we even hold back on our bright ideas when they come, for fear of blocking the bright ideas that might come from the child or adult patient. (Winnicott, 1970, p. 278, cited in Shepherd et al., 1996)

Winnicott here addresses the importance of spontaneity, which is a necessary part of creative improvisation, but the meeting between us also occurs within a social, cultural, and political arena. To meet on equal terms is an aspiration, but the meeting between practitioner and client takes place on a stage filled by cultural expectations and each participant's capacity to influence, to feel empowered or disempowered. We try to meet on equal terms but the foreground is set in many ways even before we enter the stage and meet with our clients. The meeting with another person is one that involves differential power relations. When I meet with a young client in the mental health service, I am unavoidably in a position of perceived authority. I might be seen by the client as a "mind reader" (false), a prescriber of the correct way to solve a psychological problem (false), a provider of wisdom (suspect), an agent of authority and control (possibly). These positions, and more, help to create an expectation as to what the "expert" practitioner might do. We then must consider how we might be able to usefully position ourselves in response.

We are, therefore, always on the lookout to see what "invitation" is being made to us. Do we become the supposed expert at times? Do we accept the invitation to be supportive of parents, as might a wise family elder? Sometimes, the invitation is also to be viewed with scepticism, as when a client wishes you to swear to secrecy, or presents you with an invitation that threatens professional ethics. So, to meet as human beings also includes keeping an eye on invitations that feel false or inappropriate. We can be exposed to *naïveté* if we lose our critical capacities to judge the manner of engagement offered by a client. The capacity to read the context allows us and our clients to be discerning about the degree of openness, intimacy, and trust that could fit the situation. Our responses are multi-sensorial and lead us to form impressions of one another that are felt person to person, and constantly revised through continuing exchanges and experiences. We try not to get fixed on one opinion of the other too soon. An awareness of the multi-faceted dimensions of human relatedness is part of what it means to ensure that the meeting is indeed between human beings and not between us as an experiment—though it does not exclude experimentation *within* humanising practices.

Change is inextricably bound to power relations

Systemic humanism assumes that personal change and development stem from a person's growing awareness of their active participation in dealing with challenges in life that free them from experiences of oppression. This process of development and creativity does not materialise by oppressing those who defend the status quo; the radical humanist does not resort to the oppression of others to become free. This would negate the whole process of emancipation. Instead, challenge to the status quo is considered a means by which persons "maintain alive the flame of resistance that sharpens their curiosity and stimulates their capacity for risk, for adventure, to immunize themselves against the banking system" (Freire, 1998, p. 32). "The banking system" of education is a term used by Freire to denote forms of top-down education whereby the student becomes the passive receiver of the teacher's lessons. Here, learning is considered a "deposit", so to speak, of the content that must be delivered to the student, just as one might place money in a bank. The significance of this analogy for social practices is obvious: the more practitioners are told they must follow at all costs certain imposed "pathways" for practice, the more the practitioner becomes the receptacle of the "deposit" he is obliged to comply with; this cascades down to practices with clients who are similarly caught in a "banking" system of prescribed therapies.

By contrast, the emphasis on mutuality of development places all methods, techniques, and technologies of social practices secondary to the process of mutual humanisation—a search for critically curious thinking and development that is inseparable from a recognition

> of the value of emotions, sensibility, affectivity and intuition. To know is not simply to intuit, or to have a hunch ... we must build on our intuitions, and submit them to methodical and rigorous analysis so that our curiosity becomes epistemological. (Freire, 1998, p. 48).

Freire's emphasis on learning, like therapy and other social practices, is not about separating our thinking from the feelings involved in what we do. Epistemological curiosity refers to the participant's capacity to develop critical self-reflexivity. We are encouraged to enquire into our own assumptions, allowing space for further learning and critique. This includes a socio–political analysis of our curiosity, not simply a focus on the immediate relational context but, rather, one that actively recognises where and when a client's difficulties are more accurately understood as problems of living embedded in social deprivation, injustice, and impoverishment. On occasion, we might be obliged to act on behalf of others in circumstances of high risk to life; the following example explores the ethical challenges placed before us when power *over* the other replaces power *with* the other; it is here that one's refusal to dehumanise the other is most needed and most challenged.

Power, failure, and persistence

As a social worker, I was often in the role of supervisor and monitor of families with children considered to be at risk of abuse. This meant trying to create a safe enough context for practice and support while at the same time measuring the degree of risk attached to each family's situation. This is a tricky balance; usually I found ways to connect with clients on mutually agreed aims, but not always. I recall a young mother whose two young children were removed from her by me, and eventually placed for adoption. Our social work team tried everything we could to assist the young family but somehow nothing led to an improvement for the children or the mother. Eventually, the children were admitted to hospital, having been given, by their mother, Jane, an overdose of her medication. There then ensued a lengthy debate and eventual decision to remove the children from her care. Subsequently, a drawn-out court case resulted in the children being placed with adoptive parents. Throughout the two years of work with this family I had many lengthy meetings with Jane when she sometimes sobbed and swore, got drunk, or came to see me in a desperate state of anxiety. She wept about her loss, and routinely berated me for taking her children away from her. During these periods I could count on the support of thoughtful, sensitive, and supportive colleagues who helped me not to pathologise Jane, or treat her only as a failed parent. It would have been tempting to distance myself through language that placed Jane not only as object, but also objectionable, because she frustrated and angered me at times. At other times, I felt tired out by her constant complaining and criticism. I was obliged to work within the constraints of my job as a statutory social worker, and I needed to continue to question how best to assist Jane while acting on behalf of her two young sons. Without dialogue about my ethical concerns and the wider socio–political features of Jane's plight, I doubt if I would have persisted in meeting with her. While I felt assaulted by her anger, I was also moved by her desperation and loneliness. Keeping this complexity in mind and sharing my responses with colleagues helped me to refuse to demonise Jane.

When we are under pressure and must act in ways that disempower an individual, it is tempting to evoke the oppressor inside us and treat the other in dehumanising ways. This is where good team support and supervision help humanising practices to remain at the forefront of our thinking and action. Humanisation in practice is relational, dialectical, and nurtured by the insistence of practitioners on treating one another with dignity and respect despite the "invitation" to pathologise the clients or fellow practitioners. Neither I nor my team could help Jane achieve her desire to parent her two children. In my meetings with her, I did not simply become a punch bag for Jane's verbal assaults. In time, her anger and rage also abated and allowed discussion and debate between us. Whether Jane learnt anything from our work I cannot say, but she taught me a great deal about how to refuse to objectify another human being and this learning has stayed with me throughout my career.

This example highlights ethical dilemmas that we face as practitioners. Jane's actions towards her children placed their lives in danger. The children were neglected and highly anxious, and while Jane's history and living conditions were indeed impoverished, I was obliged, ethically and professionally, to act on behalf of the children. The action of the State to remove her children, implemented by me and my colleagues, was experienced by Jane as an act of profound oppression while liberating her children from risk and potential death. Whether Jane also felt some level of relief by the decision is anybody's guess. Painful ethical decisions do not obscure ideals; in fact, they help us to value them more. To have "a profound trust in people and their creative power" (Freire, 1996, p. 56) is a belief in positive creative action towards humanity. However, it does not ignore the possibility of action that can destroy creativity in others either. Creative power is expressed in generative humanising actions that are congruent with anti-oppression. For practitioners in the social care and mental health professions, this attitude translates into ways of helping those in distress by avoiding, *where possible*, the imposition of "top-down" forms of decision making and expertise.

Contextual awareness informs responsiveness

Contextual awareness, not only self–other awareness, is the ability to sense what is called for in any given relational setting (classroom, team meeting, family therapy session); it could be described as sensing the emotional "atmosphere" when entering a dialogue with others, or even before beginning to engage with anyone. Before I deliver a workshop or seminar I like to see where I will be meeting the participants, to "feel" the room, and to notice my responses to the setting. When I meet with workshop participants, I form an overall sense of the atmosphere made up from observing others talking together, the general tone of conversation, the perceived degree of formality or informality, and the nature of my welcome. Each relational context will create an impression, a sensed response to the newly entered context. We pick up the "atmosphere" as a totality; it rests on our ability to observe our internal and external responses as we are in the act of responding, but sometimes these impressions are not so easy to express in language.

We cannot be sure at any one moment how something will turn out. But we have acute, discriminative sense that something is called for in any given context of practice.

Systemic humanism and "pearls of wisdom"

I was asked recently by a student of systemic therapy, "How do you make sense of all the historical influences that have affected the field in the last forty years or so? There are so many different approaches to learn about, and some seem incompatible with others."

I thought for a minute before saying, "It's like trying to link the various family therapy ideas as little 'pearls' of wisdom on a necklace. All the approaches, techniques, and theoretical influences are connected by a chain of influences, and the thread that links them, for me, is a systemic humanising orientation. This helps me to feel free to utilise ideas and practices from whichever source, to be useful. The family therapy pearls of wisdom are important, but the systemic humanising attitude that holds the pearls together is what unites the practice and provides a clear direction.

It is also necessary, however, to consider in detail those processes that can lead to aspects of dehumanisation that cut the thread that would connect us to co-creative practices.

Checking in with you

As I write, images from practice come back to me; I can see a child's crestfallen expression when I had to tell him I could no longer meet with him and his family. I can recall another shy teenager sitting in the waiting room looking very anxious before the first session. I remember the eyes of a mother looking for reassurance that her child was not crazy. I can recall the Polish family who brought sixteen family members to the first session, and how the energy and noise level meant I had to marshal my skills in crowd control so everybody could have their say. I also recall working with a family of a young girl with terminal cancer whose courage, and that of her family in facing the inevitability of her death was humbling. All these recollections teach me, again, about the importance of being able to bear the painful and distressing parts of our job as well as the laughter. These are human connections; they affect us emotionally. We make mistakes, and celebrate successes. There are times when I have been left with ethical dilemmas about what to do for the best. These are natural responses in a job that embraces the complexity of human connectedness. When we meet with another we meet as multi-sensorial beings with political, ideological, aesthetic, and ethical values in attendance. Our compassion for one another is crucial, and informed by our appreciation of the social conditions that oppress the development of one's creativity. Freire stresses that the pursuit of a more fully human sense of freedom is to have, "hope and optimism but not . . . false optimism or vain hope" (1998, p. 26).

What are the ideas, images and instances from your practice that come to mind and keep your creativity and commitment alive?

How do you maintain this commitment in focus to nourish your own practice?

We need to consider what it is possible to do to keep our critical curiosity alive so that we avoid vain hope and/or false optimism and, in the chapters that follow, these themes will be explored further from different vantage points.

CHAPTER TWO

Hope, and doing what is possible

The inspirational quote by El Saadawi in the Introduction emphasised that it is possible for creativity to grow despite opposition and oppression. Becoming aware that something is not right can spur one to challenge, to resist, and to ask the question, "Why is this so?" She was more than intellectually curious; her question was a provocation to herself and others not to become organised by a fear of offending the status quo. Creativity for El Saadawi includes acts of dissidence. At the same time, her provocation poses a quandary because we encounter situations with which we disagree and must decide whether to introduce a challenge to practices and policies that we consider counterproductive or detrimental to our clients. We live with frustrations when we see that more is needed to maintain humanising practices, and to connect more effectively with the clients of our services. For example, I feel angry at the over prescription of drug treatments for young children when their social and relational circumstances are the main reason for their distress. Anger is legitimate and appropriate when expressed against injustice, exploitation, and violence, yet many practitioners are required to work within systems that constrain our expressions of dissidence in the face of the restrictions on service provision. How we position ourselves, as well as how we are positioned by others, influences what might be possible (see, for example, Campbell & Groenbaek, 2006). The question is deciding how, where, and when I can act effectively, speak up, not lose heart, yet avoid false hope. Such are the expressed concerns of many colleagues I meet in social care and mental health services. So, how might we consider creative possibilities in practice without capitulation to the processes that each of us wishes to dispute and change for the better?

To try to change from within a powerful organisational system requires a great deal of attention to what one can do, as compared to what one would ideally like to do. If we become isolated in our frustrations, we are not likely to overcome them. Similarly, if creativity is isolated from engagement with others it is not likely to grow.

Becoming a possibilist

"[Hope] is not the conviction that something will turn out well, but the certainty that something makes sense regardless of how it turns out" (Havel, 1991, p. 181).

"Life without hope is hopelessly difficult but at the end hope can so easily make fools of us all" (Marsh, 2014, p. 139).

I am attending a conference organised to bring psychotherapists and ecologists together to explore common themes and practices from our respective professions. One keynote address is being delivered by a young ecologist who represents an organisation that is actively involved in trying to influence the European Union in making the case for alternative sources of energy to fossil fuels and nuclear power. The presenter offers clear evidence for the fight against global warming; he outlines the strategies he has been using to lobby policy makers and politicians from various countries. He invites questions from the audience. A delegate sitting next to me stands up to make a vociferous, emphatic comment on the speaker's presentation: "I think you are being optimistic about how change happens. Human nature, as it is, will not respond. We only respond after there has been a disaster! You are an optimist—too optimistic!"

The ecologist thinks for a moment before replying to say that he is neither optimist nor pessimist; instead, he describes what he does as the endeavours of a "possibilist". This short episode spoke to me about the need to hold on to ideals for a better world without losing heart when opposition seems to dominate. The commentator at the conference revealed his particular relationship to hope in his affirmative statement about "human nature", demonstrating how, "It is unwise to write ourselves out of the picture when we are trying to understand the moveable and changing scene of hope and hopelessness in work with clients" (Flaskas, 2007, p. 24).

At the same time, it is important to appreciate that the horizons of hope or hopelessness are largely dependent on social, political, and relational conditions with the power to either erode or build hope, feed or starve hopelessness. Hope and hopelessness can co-exist and events can spark opportunities for new hopes to emerge from feelings of despair. Byrne and McCarthy (2007) emphasise the dialectical nature of hope and despair, pointing to global catastrophic man-made or natural disasters as both, "the ground for embracing despair [and] for persevering in the face of tragedy and hoping for hope. These crisis situations highlight basic trust, the *social relation and community as the place of hope*" (p. 38, my emphasis).

When I meet with clients who appear hopeless, unable to find a way forward, or who have lost any sense of personal agency it can begin to affect me, too. I can lose energy, become bored or tired as I listen to the apparent litany of reasons why nothing can change. Perhaps they have seen several helping professionals before meeting me and, despite my exploratory questions, nothing seems to inspire possibilities for new beginnings. In these circumstances, it is perhaps understandable for practitioners to become pessimistic, especially when time is tight and imagination seems to have flown out the window.

We can also feel despair and hopelessness when demands are placed upon us through restrictive organisational practices that constrain our creative freedom. Thus, it is important to do what is possible to sustain practice and creativity, and what is possible to counter oppressive features that can be placed upon us and, in effect, tie down our practice.

The presently absent client

A boy, whom I will call David, attends a first assessment meeting in a mental health service. I am the therapist to meet with him; his mother suggests he meets me on his own at first, and I agree.

David comes to the interview room and immediately begins to cry. He cries for many minutes while I sit across from him, my head down slightly and not looking directly at him, but casting my eyes to the side, only occasionally glancing in his direction. It felt intrusive to move closer or look more directly towards him. He is fifteen years old and I think perhaps he is embarrassed by being so overcome in the presence of a stranger. I feel I should say something to ease his suffering, or at least have an idea about how to respond to him. But I resist this impulse and wait. I sit quietly, not moving much but noticing that I am taking some deep breaths, not quite sighs, but I am aware of my reaction to the boy's tears. Eventually, his tears subside; I ask, falteringly, what he would like to do. He does not say.

"Should I invite your mother to join us?" He nods.

His mother comes into the room and, seeing her son's distress, she, too, begins to cry. She talks through her agitation and tears about her deep worries for her son; his isolation, refusal to meet anyone, his depression and her own unhappiness all in a rapid flow of words that seem to have been pent up for a long time. I sit still and try to listen as the sentences tumble out. I sense the boy's sudden change of mood when he shouts in my direction, "It's not me that needs the fucking therapy—it's her!" He then stands up and leaves the room. This is the last time I see him.

Fortunately, David's mother, Sally, agreed to meet the following week and to bring her daughter and ex-husband with her, as both were equally worried about David. This was the start of a series of "think tank" sessions, as we called them; ways to experiment in responding differently to David in the hope that he, in turn, might find new ways to interact with his family.

At first this was a struggle, particularly for Sally, who had daily care of David, enduring his rages and periods of desperate vulnerability. What transpired in the think tank sessions was the strength of the family members' courage and determination to help David. I was the convenor of the sessions, sometimes mediating and facilitating the discussion but mainly encouraging their ideas to try out ways of helping David, and one another. All participants were part of the think tank team, a term which placed the working alliance between us on a more resource based footing—one in which the family's "relationship to help" was participative.

In time, with failures, mistakes, and successes encountered, the family members noted improvements in David. From time to time I sent messages to him by letter to let him know that we would continue to meet, and that the invitation for him to take part was still open. He steadfastly turned down my invitations. However, by increments, David began to venture out again, and entertain some friends at home. Within six months he accepted home tuition and the practice ended by mutual agreement within a year. During this period, Sally also began to seek help for her own troubles and made use of the think tank sessions to open discussion on changes she was already making in her own life, aside from parenting David.

Although it is impossible to capture all the features that contribute to useful, hopeful practice, the following headings seem to have general application as well as being specifically illustrative of the work with this family.

Focus on the client in his context

Of course, the fifteen-year-old boy is the named client, but from a systemic humanising orientation, the boy, the resourceful network, and the practitioner are all part of the potentially creative resource in the practice. We avoided categorising David as pathological, or his family as dysfunctional. We also managed to avoid placing him on drugs for depression or in any danger of inpatient treatment. But the practice was not usual within the constraints of the mental health service at the time; arguments were made to close the case after the first session in which the boy refused to come back. By refusing to do this I was, in effect, defining the whole relational context as the "client", that is, mother, son, father, sister, therapist, and not settling for the idea that the boy had something solely in his individual being that needed treating.

Explore personal and relational strengths

Sally began to express her reservations and self-doubts about how to alter her own behaviour in our meetings only when the think tank felt safe enough for her to show her vulnerabilities. In time, her courageous steps to try out new behaviours were coupled by changes in

Sally's view of herself; this was encouraged by all family members. It was important to follow her progress as one might accompany another person, rather than lead "from the front", so to speak. Sally's steps were faltering but too much praise from me would have sounded patronising, while too little might have been disheartening. It was more a case of gentle encouragement rather than too much celebration. This might have helped her to talk with me later without incapacitating shame about her "melt down" which had happened about three months into the sessions.

Make connections that open possibilities for useful dialogue

The invitation to focus on David's depression was what the family members brought to the table for discussion, but David, in his rage, also brought another focus: that of his wish for his mother to get help for herself. In addition, my systemic relational focus brought to the table the idea that both the boy's troubles and his mother's were connected in some way, but this idea was kept to myself until Sally started to make this connection. So, the challenge is to heed what is said by all parties and look for openings in dialogue to help mutual exploration of key concerns. Sometimes, young clients will not join in any discussion about "What is the matter", so the practitioner must find ways to respond, as with David, in such a way that his "voice" is still heard. In fact, in this example, David was engaged indirectly via the letters of invitation that informed him that we were meeting and discussing how to be of assistance.

Tread gently before making comment

We notice more than we can comment upon, so it was important not to jump into suggesting that Sally's troubles were linked to her son's. This kind of intervention usually results in clients feeling blamed by a therapist, and we might be wrong. Most parents already feel self-blame, shame, or failure when their child is so distressed.

When David began to cry, at first I thought, "In a few moments he will stop and I can gently enquire about his distress." However, he wept almost constantly for fifteen minutes. I had rarely experienced this depth and length of sobbing in a young person before, and never at the start of a first meeting. All ideas about making an assessment, filling in consent forms and the like would have been an assault on his sensibilities. I told myself to wait. But in the waiting I also wondered if I was prolonging his painful sobs; was I indulging his tears? Was I embarrassing him? All these thoughts came as I sat with him; however, I decided to remain still and silent. Noticing that I was breathing deeply in response to his sadness, the main feeling was of concern for him; the main action was to wait and see what would come. I could not know for sure how the interaction would develop but I did have an idea of what not to do.

Be available when pivotal events occur

Sally had had a very stressful weekend with David; she called it a "melt-down". She felt devastated and hopeless, and wanted to meet me as a matter of urgency.

This crisis proved to be a turning point; it was important to be available to create a meeting when desperation to change her life was most urgent; a kind of make or break time. Making time immediately available is a very real challenge for practitioners where their diaries are already full of appointments and "must go to" meetings, but this example shows that when we can be available at pivotal moments we can be more effective.

After the meeting with Sally, she became much more determined to change her life and her son's behaviour. It was as if there had been a revelation in the way she saw herself, no longer as a victim of a fearful life, but as an active actor in shaping her future, beginning to allow herself the possibility of expanding her horizon of greater knowledge. In practice, this means noticing when significant moments indicate, no matter how subtly, the possibility of a major turning point.

When Sally came to see me after her "melt-down", the meeting became a context marker that something new *must* happen if she was to make her life better for her son and herself. She saw this for the first time; both the desperate need for a change and the realisation that she had the capacity to do this. My job, at that point, was to be present to help witness and confirm this significant event as a turning point for her and our work together.

As with David and his family, the elements of systemic humanising practices are not confined to only one way of working. The basic premise is that of refusing to treat other people as objects, or as isolated from their living contexts, and instead to open possibilities for their creative power to find expression. Categories of mental distress are more fully understood as situated within a relational context, one that critiques individually focused treatments, especially where relational resources are ignored or seen as minimally significant to treatment progress. In this example, David's mother had relied on medication for depression for many years and was herself fearful of going out into the world. She felt guilty, and a failure as a parent, lost to any opportunity to see possibilities for a better life. The family was also shrouded in loss following the recent death of David's uncle through suicide, and the even more recent loss of his grandmother.

The series of think-tank sessions we devised helped the parents and their daughter to focus on how to assist David by exploring possibilities to respond differently to his aggression and bouts of desperate sadness and shame. Sally and her ex-husband also began to challenge their own ideas about how they had become victims of powerlessness. They were beginning to appreciate that transforming their relationship to David created possibilities for each participant to realise their own sense of freedom from self-oppressive ideas about having to submit to failure and impotence.

At no point was the finger of blame pointed at anyone, including David. The family members were torn between wanting to placate David because he was depressed and isolated from the world and feeling oppressed by his dictatorial demands. The think tanks focused on experimentation; doing what seemed possible without resorting to oppressive tactics in reaction to David's rages and rows. David's mother said she was ". . . always running around after him and this has to stop". David's father and mother had divorced many years earlier. Dan, his father, had been a more marginal figure in the boy's life. Now he was becoming more involved, agreed to visit David, and encourage him to go fishing with him. His sister, Veronica, supported her mother in beginning to challenge David when he was "out of order".

The work progressed, slowly by paying close attention to the achievements and set backs of each member. In this case, my focus was in keeping co-creative possibilities alive by:

- Conducting the meeting with concern for the dignity of each participant. This included holding David in mind as a child loved by his family despite his absence from sessions.

- Creating the conditions that promote the psychosocial resources in the client's network. This included an open invitation to David to join the think tank or meet with me separately; the offer to meet was the main point. As mentioned earlier, David steadfastly refused to attend but showed a growing degree of curiosity about what we talked about.

  Also important was the creation of an atmosphere of safe enough exploration of ideas in which Sally's abilities could be acknowledged. Her love and concern for her son were in the front of my mind when working with her. She eventually galvanised her resources in tackling her own fearfulness about her life, and this was supported by her ex-husband and daughter each step of the way. As part of her strategy to get help for her son, Sally encouraged neighbours, and friends of David, to visit him and invite him out. This paid off, and eventually David accepted a home schooling tutor to help pick up on his lost education. All these participants constituted the psychosocial resources in the family's network.

- Creating, with the clients, a reflective space for new learning and deepened experience. When people feel well regarded, they are more likely to allow alternative views to be entertained, both about themselves and others. The think tank does not hunt for causes or accusations of wrongdoing. People usually come to their own conclusions, in time, if an atmosphere of concerned curiosity prevails. Agreeing to explore alternative responses to David also led Sally to see a wider horizon of possibilities in her own life. This was not only an inner search for meaning, but also a jointly created exploration that emerged between participants during the sessions. This reflective space became a characteristic of the meetings that encouraged each family member to begin to think about the implications *for themselves* of the newly emerging responses to David.

- Creating an atmosphere of serious play. The atmosphere must be safe enough to improvise; it benefits from a light touch as well as the bearing of painful feelings. The idea of coming to a therapist is strange enough for most people, so it is important to make the encounter as extraordinarily ordinary as possible. A warm welcome and touches of well-timed humour help immensely, as in this case.

- Watching out for linear traps by refusing to pathologise participants for making mistakes, or failing to carry out suggestions. Self-recrimination and negativity is useful in small doses. Of course, negative feelings and pejorative descriptions occur, and can sometimes help to galvanise fresh effort: "I will never do that again. I feel so bad", but the main direction is on shifting away from the downward spiral of pejorative talk. For example, in David's case, his mother sometimes tended to put herself down: "I've lost it ... I swore at him and got drunk." To move too quickly away from the mother's expressions of failure would be a big mistake. It needs to be respected. But lingering too long in her despondency is also a mistake, because we can get drawn down into the pit of hopelessness without a ladder to climb out. Instead, it was useful to focus on ways to understand the setback without feeling all is lost. The possibilist can neither become fixed as pessimist nor cheerleader. Staying with the negativity until the opportunity arises to help further discussion is crucial. In this case, Sally would become silent as she listened to herself more. This silence was a time for quiet reflection for all of us.

The think tank was a working metaphor that fitted this family. It was a joint effort to help David, but in time David also helped himself.

The possibilist practitioner in context

This illustration sets before us the challenge to find ways to resist restrictive, uncreative, and potentially dehumanising practices. David's "case" could have been closed, as he was considered resistant to change, refusing to attend the mental health service. In contrast, a systemic humanising orientation challenges the idea of the problem being located solely within the individual.

Opening possibilities in the organisation

If the same features of "possibilism" are applied in addressing our work settings, how might they be useful to challenge restrictions on our creativity to do what is possible? Like our clients, we can be active participants in maintaining and/or challenging aspects of our working environments that are oppressive. We are not victims of circumstance, and our creative power is also worthy of realisation.

This section addresses aims for creative, possibilist practice in the work setting, mindful of the constraints that beset many services.

I begin with an example of one team's exploration to develop more creative connections in their work together.

* * *

I have been facilitating a series of training sessions in a Swedish mental health service. The series was arranged to assist practitioners in their wishes to become more effective in their therapeutic work with children and families.

The series of six days' training took place over eighteen months; during this time, the service continued to go through several changes in structure and policy implementation. We were in the flow of these changes during the period of the training sessions. Services were being compartmentalised, specialisms were being created that separated practitioners from their colleagues, and there was an increasing requirement for time-limited contacts with patients.

Further demands on time were being made in recording sessions and filling in an increasing number of bureaucratic forms. You may recognise some, if not all, of these demands in your services. However, while the impact of such policy requirements was important to acknowledge, it was also important not to get lost in feelings of hopelessness but to begin to address together what it is possible to do. It is a tricky balance to strike, because often organisational pressures are in the front of practitioners' minds. Still, the question remains—how do we keep an open mind that is alive to creative possibilities?

As the sessions developed, there was a noticeable "warming of the context" (Burnham, personal communication) with practitioners increasingly feeling freed to talk about their practice dilemmas, and to enter useful dialogue about how to work more co-operatively with each other. We had created a safe enough context to engage in discussion without recourse to unhelpful competition between disciplines.

It was significant that the managers of the service, while commissioned by the health service to implement all the organisational changes, were, themselves, supportive of commissioning our series of training days. They did not wish to constrain practitioners but they also had had their own list of "must do" instructions to implement.

The group was asked to consider some of the features of a possibilist orientation, mentioned above, and came up with the following suggestions, which were subsequently built into their organisational structure. They decided to implement more joint working, more time for supervision about clinical process (not simply case management supervision), more time built in to discussing working relationships, especially if tensions are arising, and more openness in all aspects of their practice. This emerged when one participant stated that it was very important to "Open the door to our *practice*." Another said, "It's not just open practice . . . its open *minds*."

The vision was one that incorporated diversity of opinions, skills, and approaches, without resorting to pointless rivalries between disciplines. Yet another participant said, "It's more than open practice and open minds . . . It's about open *hearts* too."

This participant spoke to the heart of the matter. What had been missing in their busy schedules was time to reflect, not only on their practice, but on their place within their team, and the care of others in the team. When caring for oneself begins to suffer, our capacity to look out for the other also diminishes. If heads go down and the computer becomes the first port of call, the focus on sustaining our collegiate connections loses its place. Isolation and emotional distance can become accomplices to dehumanising processes.

Try to create a culture of connection

In one setting, I shared a room with colleagues from child psychotherapy, clinical psychology, and art therapy. We were each trained in different theoretical models, had invested a lot of time and money in our chosen approach, and were loyal, therefore, to our prejudices about effective ways to think and practise.

Now, if we had not known each other, and were only limited to discussing abstract theories in a seminar, then, no doubt, we would have intellectualised about the merits of our chosen approach and the limitations of others. We might have dug in our heels in defence of our preferred approach. However, in the shared environment of our room, we found ways to disagree and debate without creating factions and divisions about any "true" explanation.

In this context, ideas mattered more than hierarchical positions in the organisation. Working alliances mattered more than trying to prove that one theory was better than any other. An atmosphere of creative debate developed. Students joining our informal discussions would comment on how their opinions were taken seriously. The culture created between us entertained diverse opinions in the context of mutual respect. This did not "just happen". There were several contributing features to the creative chemistry that emerged between us.

Enhancing open social mindedness

We grew to like each other. If a team member faced a painful or distressing client interview, there was nearly always someone looking out for them. It was a human connection that mattered . . . "How are you?"; "Do you fancy a coffee?"; "What would be useful to discuss following that interview?"; "You look upset" . . . or simply noticing, and waiting to allow space for the team colleague to decide to speak or remain silent, in which case the silence was also an acknowledgement of support.

"Open social minded" team relationships also grew by taking risks in sharing our vulnerabilities and uncertainties. In time, this team culture provided a vital source of support and space for critical reflection.

We all had to continue to carry out the "must dos" but they did not isolate us from one another. So often, colleagues feel they are hooked to the computer, head down and typing, trying to keep up with the paper work; they lose sight of each other. We did not feel any professional drawbridges being raised if we disagreed with each other. The computer was not the only "face" we met when we entered the room.

To be attentive towards each other also helped get us into a frame of open social-mindedness that prepared us for meeting our clients with a more open social mind, too. The atmospheric created between us helped prepare us, open our senses, so to speak, for the meetings with our clients.

We tried to maintain a culture of critical reflexivity that entertained irreverence and seriousness in equal measure. It took time, and no small degree of humility, to allow for the possibility that some of our passionately held views could be met with challenging and enlightening questions.

Discussion about why certain problems arose in clients was regarded with respect, but was overtaken by the pragmatics of what was possible to achieve. Our "team mind" was at work, not the isolated language of a definitive diagnosis, but a form of joint action that both supported each other, and pushed our thinking one step beyond our usual ways of seeing. Our theories provided potentially useful metaphors for the exploration of possibilities. How to create and maintain useful connections to the clients counted more than smart ideas about what was wrong with them.

Our team encountered conflicts of opinion but the strength of regard for each other meant that disagreements were generally seen as a sign of team solidarity. If something upset one of us it was discussed, to clear the air.

This form of team cohesion is a precious resource that needs maintenance; social rituals helped to bind relationships. So often, "good working relationships" are taken for granted, but it takes determination to maintain an atmosphere of shared respect. It is precisely this mutuality of respect that is jeopardised when practitioners are rushed off their feet, feeling like machines churning out reports to satisfy statistical returns.

Creative team work should aim for transdisciplinarity

> Transdisciplinary inquiry is not merely the additive use of knowledge from several disciplines to confront a problem, which is how I characterize interdisciplinary efforts. *Transdisciplinarity is an attitude towards enquiry as a creative process that recognizes as central the subjectivity of the inquirer and challenges the underlying organization of knowledge.* (Montouri, 2005, p. 148, my emphasis)

Montouri's research interest is in investigating creativity as a group process rather than as a quality of an individual. The emphasis is on creativity in a context. Following Bateson, "*Without* context, words and actions have no meaning at all. This is true not only of human communication in words but also of all communication whatsoever, of all mental process, of all minds . . ." (Bateson, 2002, p. 14, cited in Montouri, 2005).

In the experience of working alongside my colleagues, there were several qualities that nourished and buoyed up our informal transdisciplinary attitude to our work. I describe them here because many good intentions in team functioning are taken for granted as simply the natural, supportive, altruistic qualities we can all exhibit. Far from being insignificant, these are the binding networks of caring and supportive acts that hold teams together in a humanising endeavour towards practice.

The importance of serious playfulness and loving humour

When there are so many pressures on staff to meet organisational demands, there is great benefit in having a laugh, often at one's own expense. Sometimes, if I take my self too seriously, my colleagues' ability to "take me down a peg or two" helps me to stop and look at myself. Teasing, challenging banter knits together a camaraderie that helps counter the stressful demands of the job. The humour is not mocking or derisory; the jokes and laughter are part of the weaving of good, professional relations when they are fuelled by affection and an open heart. It is not time wasting.

Dehumanisation in the workplace happens when natural, social connection is disrupted and workers are boxed off from one another in isolated activities. Diversity stimulates thought and fresh action. We often do not know what we think until we start talking to one another. Ideas form in the process of conversation, and we might need to remind ourselves to listen to the other because they might be right. When conversation allows for fanciful ideas and light-heartedness as well as serious concerns, the quality of creativity is enhanced. We depart from the purely rational, and entertain the imagination. This context of serious play is vital for the team because it allows the practitioner to be released from tired, repetitive discussions based on formulae, or unnecessary, archaeological-style excavations to discover the supposed causes of problems.

Christopher Heimann (2009), teacher of improvisation at the Royal Academy of Dramatic Art, describes the following abilities required of an improvisational actor. I see a direct parallel in qualities for humanising practices:

> Training to become an actor is partly about undoing normal educational processes and recapturing some of our childlike abilities; the

ability to be fully absorbed in what we are doing, to be curious, vulnerable and open, truly affected by the people and things we interact with, to be present in sensorial experiences and an ability to act spontaneously and intuitively, to experience without judgement, and the ability to surprise ourselves and others.

He summarises these as the capacity that lies at the heart of his profession—the ability to play (2009). Playfulness is part of the process towards the delivery of a sensitive, imaginative but practically appropriate practice.

Encourage joint practices and let your mistakes be seen

One of the enduring benefits of training in family therapy is the way in which almost all my practice was observed, and, until very recently, joint work with a colleague or team work was a regular part of practice. Handing on skills can only be honed in direct proximity between practitioners. We also need to experience the other in practice. We do not only intellectualise about what is happening, we sense how to respond. We can learn about practice but we need to "play live", so to speak. This affords a professional, trusting, relational intimacy that bonds colleagues in joint action, in the moment-by-moment emergence of a session. There are practical benefits to joint working through shared conversation with the clients and a more transparent atmosphere for practice. Our clients experience these ways of relating openly to one another. Sometimes, an idea comes spontaneously to try out something different, and when elements of surprise, of experimentation, occur they create an atmosphere of shared endeavour between all participants. It is an invitation for creative risk-taking which clients see developing between practitioners that can rub off on the clients, too. We discuss the more experimental and performative sides of practice later, but here is a short example of such joint experimentation:

We don't know what to do for the best!

Bill and Jane are parents of Tim, aged twelve. They are deeply concerned about their son's strange and worrying behaviour in school, and now at home, where he hides himself away for hours and cannot be found, like an elaborate but strange game of Hide and Seek.

Recently, Tim tried to buy a gun from a gang member in his senior school. In discussing how to deal with the boy's risky behaviour, Bill seems to be at a loss as to how to show his concern for his son's safety. At the same time, Jane is worried that to challenge her son would make matters worse. However, both parents are anxious to try something that might address the matter of how to respond to their son.

I am in couple session with my colleague, Tessa; I ask if we could play out what we imagine might be the words to express Jane and Bill's "inner dilemmas" about what is best to do. I invite my colleague to try to speak as if from Jane's inner talk; I attempt to do the same for Bill. Tessa agrees, even though this suggestion has only come to me in the moment. The big question is whether Jane and Bill will help us by being our "critics"; to let us know if our "performance" misses the mark.

To my relief, both parents seemed cheered by the change in tone of the session towards a more experimental joint effort. They are invited to be the "consultants", so to speak; to comment on the usefulness and veracity of the "inner talk" performance. To give a flavour of the interaction here is a sample of the kind of exchange between me and my colleague; the theme briefly illustrated is based on words used by both parents earlier in the session.

> *Jim* (slightly pleading, as Bill's inner talk): The thing is, I never know what to do for the best. You see, I always try to avoid confrontations but sometimes I think Tim almost wants me to take a stand, and be much firmer in confronting him. . . . But I really think my worry for him is not shown. I keep it to myself . . . Stiff upper lip and all that.
>
> *Tessa* (as Jane's inner talk, and in a worried tone): It frightens me when you talk of confronting him. You know he goes off and hides and we don't know where he is . . . If you stand up to him we might make matters worse . . . I am always there to act as go-between between you and him when the temperature rises and I think you are going to argue with him.

This exchange continued along these lines for some minutes, interspersed with some hunches about how Tim might experience the parents if they directly discussed matters with him.

Later, the parents commented on our attempts to put across their dilemma in a sensitive manner; this, in turn, led to more open and somewhat lighter discussion about what had been stopping them from taking more action. The spontaneous role-play had allowed them to occupy a different position in the session, both as audience and critics of the therapists' "performances". Their fearfulness was explored, and the session moved to discuss their deep concern for their son. Subsequently, we were able to try some alternative responses to their son's behaviour, honed by all four of us.

The spontaneous role-play proved a useful means to open dialogue on concerns that, until the joint experiment, had become repetitive and lacking any vitality.

This example of joint work tapped the resources of the parents as well as the practitioners. It began to feel more like an equally shared exploration of how to take the next step with their son. It was not at all time consuming. Our joint work, whether in teams, as in family therapy, or co-therapy, is labour and time saving, in my experience.

Carried out well, team work with families yields fresh directions for practice and good outcomes, in contrast to the lone practitioner caught in repetitive cycles of unproductive interaction with clients because there is little or no time for critical reflection or creative comparison with another.

However, the popular view is that joint working is labour intensive and expensive—a "luxury" that can no longer be afforded. This is a false economy because, as discussed above, the cost of isolating practitioners, of creating, "silos" of separatism, diminishes creativity and co-ordinated action, and leads to burn out.

We replace processes conducive to creativity with statistics showing that more clients have been seen by fewer practitioners, but the quality of the work is not so easy to measure.

The experience of joint working encourages a more rounded discussion between practitioners where we can talk together openly about feelings, thoughts, perceptions, and associations based on our experience of working together in the same room. This is a totally different level of appreciation of practice experience from more distant talks about practice at arm's length. It allows practitioners to share nuances of the encounter with each other. We compare notes and shape ways to assist one another based on our more intersubjective experience, and appreciation of what has taken place. Anxieties are shared, and optimism often doubled, as possibilities arise. Isolated practitioners are often restricted to conversations in supervision, dilutions of the actual experience of practice, summarised for discussion, some time after the fact. Put simply, it is the difference between playing together or being limited to describing the play without being actively involved in it.

Gergen describes such attempts by groups to keep in touch with such humanising practices as "restoring the relational flow" between practitioners under pressure. This was certainly my experience within this small group of dedicated colleagues. The culture of practice we created fitted Gergen's description of

> ... forms of dialogue that attempts to cross the boundaries of meaning that locate fissures in the taken for granted realities of the disputants ... that enable participants to generate a new and more promising domain of shared meaning ... *The chief emphasis is on the process of relational coordination.* (Gergen, 2009, p. 193, my emphasis)

The practitioner with an open, social mind will remain loyal to prejudices about her preferred theories, and be able, simultaneously, to entertain doubt about her feelings of certainty.

Not everyone, however, can find it in themselves to allow a creative challenge to the way things are. Following a fellow therapist's rich case analysis and thought provoking presentation, I responded by saying, "Your description is full of wonderful metaphors that will help me in my thinking." I had hoped this would be taken as a well-intended compliment, but instead he looked at me critically and frowned as if I had deeply offended him. His idea of his chosen theoretical framework was not considered a metaphor, but a scientific truth. It was a reminder that the theories we find ourselves believing in can be held with the loyalty one might otherwise reserve for a loved family member. Offending another's family member is a risky business, and best avoided if you want to remain a companion to your colleague.

The need to nurture creativity is shown in the way practitioners behave, how they discuss their work, and treat others. This is experienced positively by others who join such a culture of relational sensitivity in face-to-face practice. Over time, such qualities of relating can become internalised, part of the repertoire of practice that is maintained and passed on. We live by example, and this rubs off on colleagues. The culture of connection is enacted, not taught.

In *Do No Harm*, Marsh (2014), the eminent neurosurgeon, talks of training surgeons over a period of thirty years, and of the importance of a hands-on approach to passing on not only the skills of the surgeon, but also the manner and demeanour that is part of the surgeon's approach to patient care.

He complains that the frequent moves of senior house surgeons mean that he no longer gets to know them as individuals or can take a personal interest in their careers. The same can be described in mental health services, when colleagues are employed on short-term contracts where their knowledge of clients is limited. This affects team cohesion and morale. "Here today and gone tomorrow" is the expressed concern of clients who see several therapists during their treatment. Team members feel the same way. How can you challenge and support a colleague whom you do not know well enough to tease or correct in ways that would not damage relations? This takes time and a good dose of mutual respect.

Here is Marsh talking about a similar process where he describes the importance of irreverent meetings as a source of staff support. These early morning meetings with his colleagues were

> not like the dull and humourless hospital management meetings where there is talk of keeping in the loop about the latest targets or of feeling comfortable about the new Care Pathways. Our neurological morning meeting is a different sort of affair. Every day at eight o'clock sharp, in the dark and windowless x-ray viewing room, we shout and argue and laugh while looking at the brain scan of our poor patients and crack black jokes at their expense. (p. 16)

The humour is contextualised by the deep professional care that comes with the dedication to good practice. The irreverent jokes assist thinking, team cohesion relieves anxiety, and acts as a warm up for the day ahead. It sustains us.

I am *not* advocating a form of humour in practice that dehumanises or objectifies our clients. Humour should be witty, and, at best, self-deprecating, but it is also the case that we can permit a dose of irreverence so long as it is appreciated that the care and dignity of those we work with is uppermost in our concerns. We are not laughing *at* the other, but often at *ourselves*, or *with* the other.

Reflections on possible steps and possible trips

What could be the small but significant changes/challenges that could make for a "not too unusual difference" in your practice?

How could challenges be made while respecting the dignity of others?

How could the resourceful contexts within your workplace be mobilised in more creative directions?

How could preservation of the reflective space be made, and are there opportunities for the serious play of ideas and diversity of thought between you and your colleagues?

Are there avenues open to challenge restrictive practices and restrictive language of pathologies and dysfunction as descriptors of service users?

What conditions allow us to continue, like Sally, to keep hope alive?

These are big questions that are explored in the forthcoming chapters. Each step has its consequences, but not to take a step leaves us resigned to the status quo.

As a consultant in the National Health Service (NHS), I had a stronger voice than others in proposing suggestions for changes within the supervisory contexts in our mental health team. I could be more outspoken about policies with which I disagreed. However, one's influence within any work setting will be affected by dominant ideas about what constitutes the "must dos" of policy and administrative procedures. The influence we might try to exert in attempting to challenge and redirect priorities can become an irritant or a threat to those who are implementing procedures one might disagree with.

If I speak out repeatedly against certain dominant ideas, I could become marginalised by being considered as either a critical "backbench" member of the opposition and/or spokesperson on behalf of those more cautious about criticising agency policies. Either way, I am in a difficult position; I am obliged to comply with certain "must dos" to keep my job, but I also need to speak about those policies that I find contradict humanising practices. This is a dialectical position in which debate about ideas and practices is necessary because we have a vision of what we stand for in upholding effective, humanising practice. This includes: how do we creatively disobey?

Disobedience ... is an act of the affirmation of reason and will. It is not primarily an attitude directed against something, but for something: for man's capacity to see, to say what he sees and to refuse to say what he does not see. To do so he does not need to be aggressive or rebellious; he needs to have his eyes open, to be fully awake and willing to take responsibility to open the eyes of those who are in danger of perishing because they are half asleep. (Fromm, 1981, p. 24)

In the next chapter, we look more into the ideas and conditions under which creative practice can be developed, both within our work settings and in our relationship to our personal style of work. We explore those ideas and features of practice that can, and do, inspire us. We also ponder how to creatively challenge the status quo when the status quo restricts the voices of challenge, hope, and possibility.

CHAPTER THREE

Exploring creativity in context

There is a story told by the late John Weakland, from the Brief Therapy Centre (Fisch et al., 1982; Watzlawick et al., 1974), who was inspired by a client's distinction between a difficulty and a problem in life. According to Weakland, the client defined the distinction thus: "A difficulty is just one damn thing after another . . . A problem is the same damn thing time and time again!"

When we are caught up in repetitive and unproductive processes in our work, it is easy to see how we can become disillusioned and resigned to follow the increasing demands on our energy and willingness to continue to do a good job. This chapter invites your exploration of what can, and does, provide us with inspiration by looking at dimensions of practice that open possibilities for continued development and inspiration. This is a way of setting aside some time to reflect on what matters to us as practitioners. It is a breathing space. It is also a chance to consider your unique ways of developing your creativity, yet avoiding the illusion of thinking that one's creativity comes only from within, as if by magic. A systemic humanising perspective places creativity as a psychosocial process, aided or restricted by our living relations with others, and our historical precedents.

Creativity and the practitioner's development

The following three dimensions for development present an opportunity for you to pause, and allow time to think about what contributes towards more creative practice for you. I invite exploration here of how our search for knowledge and inspiration finds expression in our work, taking account of the conditions that threaten to stifle creative potential.

Reaching towards creative practices involves an exploration of what we find stimulating and satisfying in the jobs we do; the three dimensions set out here provide an opportunity to think about the interrelations between our knowledge in its various forms, the development of our individual style (that is, what we *do* with knowledge) and how we maintain a spirit of generosity towards ourselves and others. All three dimensions are mutually influential. They are in conversation with one another.

To illustrate the dimensions in a workshop, I invited three participants from the audience to sit together as personifications of each of the three dimensions named: Knowledge, Style, and Generous Spirit. Having outlined the features of the seated three, a member of the audience suggested that the characters were too static. Acting on this, I invited the three characters to discuss how they would prefer to arrange themselves. After a brief discussion, they created a ring, holding hands and moving, as in a movement of co–creativity reminiscent of Matisse's *The Dance*. This was a much livelier portrayal of mutual influence than anything I could come up with.

When I invite workshop participants to discuss the influence of the three dimensions upon their practice, I have regularly noted colleagues from different disciplines talking openly together in their search to make fresh connections about the values they share that led them into this work in the first place. Explorations of this type move beyond the all-too-common focus on the technology of practice, the busyness of dealing with more administrative procedures and measurements of one sort or another. Instead, the focus settles on what unites practitioners from different theoretical backgrounds in their search to do a better job. To be open socially minded is to become less partisan about divisions between disciplines, theoretical orientations, and professional competitiveness by refocusing on our work as a human endeavour, and the ethics that underpin practice as a process of humanisation.

As you read through this section, I would encourage you to pause and consider for yourself the importance of forms of knowledge that inspire you, and give yourself some time to celebrate your unique abilities and style as a practitioner. It is not about self-congratulation, more a matter of realising all the important influences upon you that can all too easily be overlooked in the busyness of daily practice. In addition, the exercise at the end of this chapter encourages a further exploration of creativity that can best be carried out in groups of three. It is usually best to do this exercise with some trusted colleagues, or even invite colleagues you would like to get to know better to try it with you.

Knowledge, style, and a generous spirit

The idea for the three dimensions came about when a friend bought me a book titled *Guitar Man* (Hodgkinson, 2006). The gist of the narrative is to take the reader through the various stages the author, Will Hodgkinson, had made in his attempt to learn to play the guitar as an absolute beginner. The aim was to be able to perform before friends and family within six months of picking up the guitar for the first time. Near the beginning of his quest, he identified three elements of development (themselves borrowed from the writing of St Augustine) these being knowledge, style, and a generous spirit (originally grace). Each of the dimensions is in circulation with the others, and shapes their further development.

Here, I describe the idea in more detail to help focus attention on the different forms of knowledge and their expression in practice.

Intellectual knowledge

This consists of all the studies we have made in our professional lives: the theories that inspire us, the concepts that have stood the test of time, and the texts that have stood out as sustaining our creativity in thinking. Knowledge that comes from intellectual stimulation will include the vast array of studies from other sources: music, literature, art, philosophy, poetry, in fact, any endeavour or fascination that we find intellectually sustaining during our lives. This intellectual stimulation helps contribute to our repertoire of thought, thus having a bearing on our practice. This we can call "head" knowledge, and is like musicians' need to study some music theory, know something of scales and chord sequences, perhaps also to learn to read music.

However, training in certain approaches to therapy can marginalise areas of the practitioner's life that could otherwise be brought into their practice. A family therapist who watched me play on the floor in a family therapy session with children told me how perturbed he was at seeing me use "play techniques". He had once trained as a play therapist and then retrained to become a family therapist. When he completed his family therapy training he felt he had to put aside all the experience he had gained as a play therapist. He had pigeonholed the two separate trainings, believing that it would be inauthentic and incompatible to use ideas and practices from his previous experience in his current practice as a family therapist. This is an example of how professional training can create restrictive repertoires in its drive to define model-congruent practices. Of course, it is common practice to suspend our habitual ways of thinking and acting when we try to acquire new skills, but this colleague had completely shelved his prior skills repertoire for many years; he had adopted a way of thinking and behaving that divorced him from his wider knowledge base and creativity.

Knowledge gained through observation

This type of knowledge includes watching practitioners at work, learning from joint work, teamwork, and "master" classes. It is akin to the musician who watches other performers and absorbs their techniques to transform musical notation into live music. The musician copies, mimics, and rehearses new forms and musical patterns as a way to incorporate new learning into her own repertoire, as in jazz improvisation (Barrett, 2012). First comes the copying; then comes originality.

When I studied the family therapy of Gianfranco Cecchin in the mid 1980s, I watched and tried to emulate his way of interviewing families. I did this over a two-year period. Each month I would study with him for two days. When I returned to work, my colleagues could always tell that I had been studying with Cecchin because I was using his gestures and shoulder movements when I met with the client families. It was a clear case of hoping to absorb the magic of the "expert" by copying his every move. Fortunately, this devoted mimicry faded in time. It is not problematic to do this; it *is* problematic if you get stuck in trying to emulate the expert because you will never find your own style.

Sensorial knowledge

This is knowledge that comes from paying attention to one's embodied responsiveness (Seikkula & Arnkil, 2014). For the practitioner, this is gained through attending to feelings that can be transient, letting such embodied responses inform meaning without rushing to explain away the feelings that emerge.

> From a removed perspective, you can divide [an interaction] . . . into separate components; affects, cognitions, and a sequence of actions, perceptions as well as sensations. Each can be looked at separately. But First Person experience is not broken up like that; it is felt as a whole. (Stern, 2004, p. 35)

Stern points to the significance of the practitioner's attention to sensed responsiveness. We are multi-sensorial beings and, in concert with a generous spirit, every sense is brought to bear on our meeting with the clients. Having a sense of the other comes with the knowledge that our embodied responses are sometimes hard to articulate but we have a "feel" for how to go on in an encounter. If we dismiss our sensed hunches, we miss an opportunity to experience their potential usefulness for the meeting between us and the other. Embodied experience is valued even when we cannot precisely explain why a certain feeling has come to us. Sensed hunches that are dismissed or not given sufficient thought and time for exploration might later be made clear as subsequent events unfold and leave us wishing we had acted more directly on our sense that something did not sit well with us.

I recall meeting a client who was covertly critical of my ability as a therapist, tolerating my presence but keeping a distance from me. I had a sense that he was throwing me rehearsed lines in his replies to my questions. I noticed how I felt awkward in his company; the rhythm of my responses to him was stilted, and my breathing less relaxed than usual. In short, I felt uneasy in his company, and it was only after discussing my embodied responses with my colleagues that

I began to find a more useful direction in my future meetings with him. Naming and exploring my hunches and associated feelings gave me an opportunity to reflect and alter my responses. In so doing, my hunch about him could more readily be addressed. When we do not explore such felt experiences, we can miss opportunities to open new possible directions in practice. It helped to begin to talk with him about my impressions of his holding back in our sessions. He then began to talk of his apprehension about discussing painful matters in his life. Addressing the hunch helped to address what was unsaid, yet present, in my experience of the previous session.

A boy I worked with had been placed in a boarding school for children with behavioural problems. When I first visited the school, I felt somehow uneasy about the headmaster and headmistress, who seemed too well mannered and too contained. The schoolteachers I met seemed rather distant and cowed by the head staff. Everything was *too* polite and ordered. The children I met were too polite; all the school rooms were too clean and tidy for my liking. However, I had no reason to suspect any wrongdoing despite my unease about the atmosphere in the school. Some years later, I discovered that the head teachers had been prosecuted for sexually abusing some of the children in the school. I had missed an opportunity to discuss my hunch with others by letting it slip away in my busy practice. Hunches can be wrong, but they do warrant attention.

Knowledge from a community of minds

We are born into a community of minds. As Tallis (2012) puts it, "we humans are caught up in a boundless nexus of knowledge, and relate to the culture sustained by a community of minds, rather than being wired directly into nature" (p. 187).

The meaning given to our sensory responses is expressed in language provided by our particular community of minds. Our class, culture, gender, and abilities affect how we define ourselves, and are defined by others; our values are recursively created and expressed in our daily lives. These values can be considered our personal prejudices (Cecchin et al., 1994) and can make a useful contribution to our practice. They can also become obstructions if they are imposed on other people without careful consideration. Pontificating about the right way to live places a responsibility to live up to one's preaching.

Instead of trying to live like a saint, the practitioner's task is to consider how our lived experience, our values, and our prejudices, affect our practice, and to be mindful that our strongly held beliefs can be useful in certain contexts, and damaging in others.

Countering troublesome prejudices is difficult to do but, if they are open to scrutiny and modification, they can really assist our thinking. Our lived experience provides an implicit, relational map of how we act, react, and respond in the world around us. In this context, the importance of this form of knowledge is, first, to assist us in comparing our experience with the others we meet, and second, by exploring the way such knowledge can be put to use. Systemic humility places us in relation to our passionate ideas without letting them dictate to others. When Freire states that without humility there cannot be dialogue, he is not eschewing debate, but he is advocating that

> Whoever has something worth saying has also the right and the duty to say it. Conversely it is also obvious that those who have something to say should know that they are not the only ones with ideas and opinions that need to be expressed. Even more than that, they should be conscious that, no matter how important the issue, their opinion probably will not be the one truth long and anxiously waited for by the multitudes. (2001, p. 105)

Knowledge about how we come to know

Critical self-reflexivity encourages exploration about the stand we take on matters. It helps us to entertain a degree of doubt by paying attention to the limitations and the usefulness of what we know. As human beings, we can think about our thinking. We are in a reflexive relationship to the forms of knowledge outlined above. This reflexivity includes attention to our moral values, our prejudices, and our passionate beliefs. Through our attention to knowledge that informs and forms our development as sentient beings, we have the capacity to grow and develop. Knowledge grows with our capacity to question and reappraise our ways of thinking.

Socrates remarked, "All I know is that I know nothing". Pyrrhonian scepticism starts from this point, but then adds, in effect, "... and I'm not even sure about that" (Bakewell, 2011, p. 124).

As a social worker, many years ago, I often had to deal with cases of physical neglect and emotional abuse of children. I look back on those days and think that our service cared deeply for the children and families we worked with. At the same time, the incidence of reported, disclosed, or investigated sexual abuse was almost unheard of. We were not intentionally negligent practitioners. However, we were operating within a dominant societal and organisational discourse that did not recognise the signs of sexual abuse. This was not a "cover up"; it was not within the ken of the service. So, our knowledge is always qualified by what is not known. Consider for a moment that all your knowledge as a practitioner is placed in a circle, the circumference of which marks the limits of your knowledge. As you progress and gain more experience, the circle expands and, of course, so does the circumference of what you do not know. The more we learn, the more we are in touch with what is still unknown. In our social services team, we were ignorant of what was happening to children who were abused sexually. Later, when reports of sexual abuse came to light, we became more aware of what was always present but unseen. Our knowledge increases but it leaves us with the humbling thought that our current practice is likely to have similar blind spots; it is important, therefore, to take a position of uncertainty about any idea of final, stable knowledge. Knowledge is a spur to exploration as well as a process of discovery.

Our relationship to knowledge is open-ended. The practitioner who can take constructive criticism, and pay close attention to feedback from clients is very likely to improve his or her performance. Miller and Hubble propose that our development requires "consistently and consciously pushing to reach objectives just beyond one's level of proficiency (2011, p. 25).

For the musician, intellectual study of musical theory can help create structure to his learning. Observation of other musicians helps him to appreciate and understand how more experienced musicians' playing is more refined and nuanced. The budding musician enters the culture of musicians, learns the language of musicianship, and absorbs the history of different musical genres. However, at some point in the search for more knowledge, the beginner must pick up the instrument and play. He has now made a leap into the risky domain by trying out his fledgling knowledge. He must *do* something. This dimension of development is called our style.

Style is unique. No one will be able to practise the way you do. Style is always in a process of development; it is never fixed. The realisation that each practitioner will have their own unique styles of practice is liberating and opens opportunities to best connect with the style and repertoire of the clients we meet. Sometimes, we accompany the client, supporting their style, and sometimes we intervene more to take the lead for a while. All of this is like an improvisation, playing in accordance to what is required of the moment.

A jazz musician will listen to, then copy, other musicians' phrasing. Certainly, it can be useful if you decide to copy other practitioners for a while, as I did with Cecchin, but the creative jazz musician who listens then copies other musicians' phrasing in the end will play the music in his own style. The uniqueness of one's own style also debunks the myth that to slavishly follow the directives of the expert will capture their unique "magic".

On the contrary, the realisation that your style is unique frees you to look more closely to home in pursuing creativity and development. It pushes us to realise our own creative potential. Put simply, style is *how* we put knowledge to work and *what* we do constitutes our repertoire of practice which can always expand, just as a professional musician learns to play in different musical modes depending on what is asked of her.

Repertoires expand or contract depending on one's working context. I recall my first tentative steps in working with couples referred with sexual problems. My style was awkward; my repertoire of ways to explore sexual difficulties was embarrassingly mechanistic in execution. Nevertheless, with increased knowledge, application, and a growing degree of familiarity with the topic of sexual difficulties, I began to feel a little more at ease. I think my clients had a very generous attitude towards my first, fumbling attempts to discuss such intimate matters.

Gurus can be useful for a while

Eric Clapton is a musical hero of mine; I have followed his music for many years and I admire his guitar playing and much of his songwriting. As chance would have it, I bumped into him some years ago, and was overawed at meeting "God" face to face. ("Clapton is God" was a popular description of him by fans in the 1960s.) In the awkward moment that followed, I said, "Hello Eric . . . How are you doing?" He nodded, and crossed the road, leaving me stunned and wondering, "Was that really him?" It was, of course, and, despite my awe-struck response, I also noticed how much taller I was than him and that his skin was tired looking. Perhaps it is a good idea, when coming face to face with "God", to realise s/he is a mortal soul after all. I realise I will never play guitar like Eric but I can improve how I play like me.

When the musician learns how to play proficiently, her style will begin to emerge and, with practice and experimentation, her repertoire will grow. Development involves both excitement and a degree of risk. To develop one's style means both practising and making mistakes. The aim is to liberate practice from the confines of empty repetition and formulaic responses. If our style becomes fixed, and we are too certain of the direction we should take, it will lack spontaneity and a degree of improvisation. To develop our style is to try to transcend our usual ways of practice, and to release creativity in the context of our work with clients.

Each practitioner's style is unique and always open to development. The late Tom Andersen (1990) had a gentle, quiet voice but a strong presence; his delivery was slow and precise. I had the pleasure of working with Tom from time to time over several years when he visited our Institute. My style is more active, more expressive in gesture and manner than Tom's, but the point is we somehow managed to work together in useful ways. Each of our styles had a different texture woven with a common thread of a shared humanising orientation. If you have one preferred style, you can enhance this by working with others whose style is different in order to learn more, expand possibilities for clients, and increase your own practice repertoire.

A generous spirit

Courage and caring curiosity

To take steps to experiment and be prepared to fail requires a certain amount of courage, or "wise fear". Acting with wise fear is done because of our belief that matters will turn out better than if we refused to act. It requires a generous attitude towards the other, whereby we hope that an act of generosity imbued with curiosity and care will be recognised as such and appreciated by the other. Courage, in this sense, is not about fearlessness but wise fear. To take a calculated risk in practice requires an attitude that welcomes uncertainty in the belief that such a step will bring with it a degree of hope and new possibility. This attitude of spirited practice is like the "feel" a musician brings to his playing; it is something beyond technique, something that conveys an emotional engagement with the music, transcending mere repetition of the notes. It has soul. You can listen to two different renditions of the same piece of music and the spirit in which the music is played will somehow be sensed by you. One piece could register in you as if the musician is "going through the motions", while the other rendition might stir you as the soulfulness of the playing touches you. Admittedly, this is a subjective judgement, but a generous spirit is a crucial third pillar for development as a practitioner. This is what clients seem to pick up when they meet the practitioner. The connection goes beyond words. It is sensed in the manner in the moment of meeting.

To work with a generous spirit is not a fixed quality. It is bolstered by attention to the various forms of knowledge we acquire, and the care taken towards the other when we put ideas into practice. Of course, this is not a linear process; the style and repertoire of the practitioner are in conversation with knowledge. One's generosity of spirit is enhanced or diminished by how one can express personal style and relish one's knowledge. Yet, knowledge is not always consciously present in our interactions, as in the following example of a moment of meeting with a client.

The handshake: a meeting of two nervous people

I receive a phone call from a social work colleague. She tells me that one of my supervisees had met a family for a first session recently and that she was also involved in the case. The father is with her in her office when she calls me. He had been complaining about the poor service his son had so far received from the police, social services, and the CAMHS service. She anxiously requests that the father be seen urgently, as he is threatening to assault staff unless his son gets to see a therapist immediately.

I know nothing of the situation. The allocated therapist is on holiday, and this is a new case not yet discussed in supervision. However, I note the urgency in the social worker's voice and I ask if she could invite the father, Mr Harvey, to meet with me the next day. I ask her to ask him to please bring his son because he is so concerned about him. The social worker conveys the message and I receive confirmation that Mr Harvey will come to see me the following morning.

On my way to work the next day, I was thinking about the coming meeting; this angry man who has had a bad experience with practitioners and the police is likely to come to the meeting expecting an argument, and to fight for the cause of his son. I recall other such tense first encounters, but somehow experience of this kind does not make the tight feeling in my stomach disappear.

I receive a call from reception to say that Mr Harvey has arrived twenty minutes early, and is pacing the corridor outside the waiting room. What to do? I take a deep breath. I tell myself I must do a professional job so I advance towards the corridor where I see that Mr Harvey is a good three inches taller than me. He is looking at a notice on the wall as I approach. I walk up to him and say with as much clear and confident diction as I can muster, "Hello Mr Harvey; my name is Jim Wilson."

I hold out my hand to shake his hand and, as he meets my eyes, our hands clasp. At that moment, I do not see anger in his eyes, but confusion. I also think that I sense sadness as his gaze drops. The handshake is firm, perhaps too firm, and I explain that I will meet with him in a few minutes.

As I approached Mr Harvey, I did not call upon knowledge drawn from theories but from my embodied response first to the phone call and to seeing this tall, agitated man respond to the offer of my hand. At each moment, we responded to each other in a way that could not be preordained. I had an expectation that he might shout or rant or even physically threaten me, but as I approached I let that thought slip, and instead decided to welcome him into the waiting room.

Of course, we can theorise about this after the fact—was I attempting to de-escalate aggressive interaction by deciding to respond in a way that counters his expectation of opposition? Or was I effectively trying to reframe Mr Harvey's aggressive responses as a sign of his care and concern for his son.

Stern considers such moments as the handshake to be more fully comprehended as existing outside linear time.

> It is the coming into being of a new state of things, and it happens in a moment of awareness. It has its own boundaries, and escapes or

transcends the passage of linear time. . . . It is a subjective parenthesis set off from chronos. *Kairos* is a moment of opportunity, when events demand action or are propitious for action. Events have come together in this moment and the meeting enters awareness such that action must be taken, now, to alter one's destiny—be it for the next minute or a lifetime . . . It is a small window of becoming and opportunity. (2004, p. 7)

I am not sure how the handshake quite altered our destinies, but it was a very important beginning connection. I also noticed in Mr Harvey's hesitant response to me a glimmer of generosity, and a generous attitude to others is also an act of kindness.

To live well we must be able to imaginatively identify with other people, and allow them to identify with us. Unkindness involves a failure of the imagination so acute that it threatens not just our happiness but our sanity. Caring about others . . . is what makes us fully human. (Phillips & Taylor, 2009, p. 97)

The curiosity of the systemic practitioner should be imbued with caring towards the other. Curiosity has the Latin root for care, *cura*, meaning (among other definitions) concern (for), attention (to) (*Collins Latin Dictionary and Grammar*, 1997). I interviewed Cecchin some years after his highly influential article exploring curiosity (1987) had become a central guiding concept for many systemic therapists. When asked by me if he thought his practice style had changed over the years, he said he thought that he had become "a little warmer". His curiosity involved caring, but he did not make his expression of caring a smothering kind; it avoided oversentimentality. It was in the service of being "useful" rather than "helpful", the latter being connected in his mind to being overly involved emotionally with the clients. He was always vigilant about not being stuck in one emotional stance or conceptual idea. Caring curiosity is expressed in different ways as per the perceived requirements of the relational context, and each of us will have our own style in expressing how we "do" caring curiosity.

Knowledge, style, and generosity of spirit are context dependent; aspects of them are evoked in response to circumstance. In time, they become features of our development, and operate beyond any simple description of what we do.

Just as the musician must learn to accompany others in enhancing the performance, so the practitioner must find ways to enhance the possibilities in working with clients. It is *their* creativity that counts, and our job is to ensure this aim is uppermost in our minds.

When our spirit is diminished, or our curiosity to engage in fresh ideas is lost, we lose our creative urge and practice becomes bereft of effort.

Creativity as resistance to oppressive practices

Afuape, writing on liberation psychology, considers, as do Freire and El Saadawi, that creativity can be an expression of resistance to oppression: "Creativity as an alternative metaphor for resistance might mean we are less inclined to kill off the need for resistance in our lives and in the therapeutic relationship". Resistance can be viewed as the emergent expression of freedom of thought and action, "as it is based on hopes of how things should be" (2011, p. 195).

She suggests that artistic expression can be an effective form of resistance to oppression, such as in soulful singing for example, where victimhood is sloped off, and liberation is felt when the singer evokes the sense that "the world does not have full power over [us]" (Afuape, 2011, p. 196).

The correspondence between systemic humanising practices and the search for creativity can be considered as a form of liberation from the oppressive constraints on practice that confine both client and practitioner. The effect of changes in the provision of social care and mental health will be fully addressed in detail in Chapter Six, and includes the effect of commodification of services and the implications of evidence-based practices; that is, where *outcome* of therapeutic services is measured as a function of *income* and cost. These macro-political influences profoundly affect the micro-politics of working life in the ways we choose to relate to one another. For now, I simply wish to bring these matters to the table in relation to constraints on creativity in context.

In the following exercise, our relationship to creativity in context is explored.

Creativity: individual and collective expressions

In Montouri and Purser's (2000) study of co-creativity, their search for the collaborative and social dimensions of creativity rejects the popular dichotomy that isolates creativity from collective expression; instead, they argue that creative processes are sparked by many actors and events, through either chance or deliberate actions. The idea that creativity is ninety per cent perspiration and ten per cent inspiration is not so far from the truth, but the sweat of toil is produced by many.

There is, however, something of a paradox in proposing creativity as only a collective endeavour, since creativity also requires some sense of personal creative investment in its expression.

There is a scene from the satirical film *The Life of Brian* in which Brian, who is mistaken for the Messiah, protests to the assembled and deluded followers that he is in fact *not* the Messiah. In desperation, he appeals to them, "You are all individuals!" only to receive the resounding response, "We are all individuals!" One hesitant member of the devotional assemblage raises his arm and says, in a reluctant, feeble voice . . . "I'm not."

Creativity simply placed in opposition to conformity implies a division between "creative types" who might disrupt the organisational structure and process and conforming individuals who fit into the bureaucratic order and can be controlled. We are all capable of taking different positions at different times; creativity is performed and experienced in many ways, informed by the interplay between political, personal, methodological, and perceptual considerations.

Creativity and aesthetics of practice

Creative practices afford recognition of differential skills and capacities from each participant in a project, guided by principles of systemic humility, systemic awareness, and a belief in the creative power of each person.

Creativity is the emergence of an aesthetic process initially hidden from view and smouldering away until it sparks into life. Thereafter, the visible expression of creativity gathers momentum.

The protest songs of Woody Guthrie, or black soul singers, provided inspiration to accompany the marchers for civil rights in America. These forms of creative expression have roots in earlier, latent processes.

"Strange Fruit": a case in point

> Black bodies swinging in the southern breeze,
> Strange fruit hanging from the poplar trees . . .

Abel Metropole wrote "Strange Fruit" first as a poem, published in 1937. He was a schoolteacher from the Bronx, committed to American civil rights. He was horrified when he first saw photographs of the lynching of black men. Metropole introduced the poem to Billie Holliday at an integrated nightclub in New York, but she did not appreciate the import of it until after the poem was put to music. This involved arrangers, producers, sound engineers, and musicians being invested in the song's evolution. In time, via radio broadcasts, the public was exposed to the special quality of the song and one million copies had sold by 1939.

Creative expression took shape in ways that avoided oppressive practices. The beginnings of the creative process are impossible to define, but from personal protest against lynching, the generative process was fanned out by all the others involved. Creativity is not an isolated event. The boundaries of creativity are not easily defined but are grown in contexts, often of opposition to prevailing power and influence.

> Protest implies the existence of formal, political channels through which dissent can be collectively expressed. In this context, protest would suggest some strategic goal, such as bringing black women domestic workers into organised trade unions. But such a historical possibility did not exist at the time. Protest *when expressed through aesthetic forms* is rarely a direct call to action. Nevertheless, critical, aesthetic representation of a social problem must be understood as constituting powerful social and political acts . . . a form of contestation of oppressive conditions, even when it lacks a dimension of organised political protest. (Davis 1998 p. 101). (Afuape, 2011, p. 196, my emphasis)

Co-creativity: the ability to remain social minded

When I was preparing for a seminar on creativity in psychotherapy, the radio was on and, as chance would have it, a programme discussing the jazz classic by Miles Davis, "A Kind of Blue" was being transmitted. I stopped and listened to some old recordings of interviews with the great jazz player. When he was asked about the special quality of the album, I began making notes from his response. In the salient points that follow about what is important in co-creativity, for "music" and "musician", read "practice" and "practitioner".

- Choose musicians that complement each other, as they will bring different abilities and scope to the music.
- Don't write overly complex forms of music; keep structures simple, as that way there is more space to improvise.
- Don't try to repeat what has been played. Each performance is unique.

To find colleagues you can work with who have different ways of putting their thinking into practice can be inspiring so long as each participant has the capacity for humility towards their ideas, and enough openness to have them challenged without pride getting in the way.

Here is a diary entry by the British playwright and actor, Alan Bennett, which captures the attitude of creative co-operation:

> 27th June. To a recording studio at the BBC to lay down music tracks for a short film I have written about Proust. . . . Striking about the musicians is their total absence of self-importance. They play a passage, listen to it back, then give each other notes, and run over sections again. . . . David H., the director chips in too, but he isn't a musician, just knows what atmosphere he wants at various points in the film. In the finish, even I chip in, just because I know what I like. And the musicians nod and listen, try out a few bars here and there, then settle down and have another go—now, one could never do this with actors. No actor would tolerate a fellow performer who ventured to comment on what he or she was doing—comment of that sort solely coming from the director, and even then, it has to be carefully packaged and seasoned with plenty of love and appreciation. Whereas these players, all of them first-class, seem happy to listen to the views of anyone if it results in them doing a better job. (2006, p. 263)

Creativity: constraints and possibilities, a workshop exercise

This is designed to explore restrictions and possibilities in one's context of practice. If time permits, you might like to try this exercise with the help of two colleagues. You are asked to explore the theme of creativity in your practice, both its expression and the constraints placed upon it.

Here are the steps.

Exploring the presence of creativity

Participants are divided into groups of three, with one person agreeing to present their "relationship to creativity" while another facilitates this presentation; the third member of the group takes on the character of the presenter's creativity as in a role-play.

The exercise begins with an appreciative enquiry about creativity; the presenter is asked questions to encourage exploration of their own creative possibilities; for example,

- When is your creativity alive and well in your practice?
- When present, how does creativity show itself?
- On what occasions are you aware that creativity is fully with you?
- How do you feel/think/behave then?
- What are the main features in the context (family interview, couple session, supervision) which are conducive to creativity lending a hand?

The facilitator *ad libs* questions as seem appropriate until the positive expression of creativity is explored thoroughly. All this time, the character of Creativity is sitting aside, listening and noticing their reactions and responses to the conversation as it evolves.

The only tip here is for the person role-playing Creativity to suspend their own feelings about creativity and, instead, allow him- or herself to be moved in response to what is heard. In effect, that person is bringing the character of Creativity to life as he/she listens. It is an exercise of the imagination. It requires close attention to listening and responding. The only stipulation is that Creativity is a *benign influence* on the presenter, since it is already a part of the presenter's repertoire, and, therefore has good intentions towards the presenter.

Exploring constraints

After perhaps ten minutes, the facilitator "turns over the coin" to explore the constraints on creativity to be described by the presenter. Again, the character of Creativity listens and notices his/her responses as the conversation develops. Typical questions are:

- When your creativity is most distant from you, what sorts of situations come to mind?
- How does the absence of your creativity affect your thinking/action/feelings?
- Are there particular situations/types of work where your creativity is least present?
- How come creativity leaves you behind at these times?

These are sample questions, and, therefore, in no way comprise an exhaustive list. The main point for the facilitator is to create a manner of discussion of creativity as *a personification*. This helps the person role-playing Creativity to get a better sense of embodying the character. It begins to feel alive and "real". Externalising type questions assist here, but any form of question that allows the presenter to continue to talk about Creativity as a separate character is useful. What typically begins to happen is that the presenter begins to see their creativity as a relational feature of their style and repertoire as a practitioner, and to appreciate how creativity is powerfully affected by the context of one's practice.

Inviting hypothetical future possibilities

The third exploratory form of questions asks the presenter to imagine:

- If creativity were more actively involved in your practice in the future, how would its presence be felt?
- How would it show itself in your repertoire of practice?
- What conditions (small steps) could contribute to this possibility becoming more of a reality?

Such a form of questioning allows for a more realistic appraisal of what could be introduced while taking account of the real-life constraints of the presenter's practice setting.

Invite Creativity to respond

After the three contexts of creativity have been explored, the facilitator then interviews Creativity in character. Here, Creativity is asked only to talk in the first person, that is, in character. That way, the person role-playing Creativity has free rein to improvise based on the experience of listening in (with every sense), from the observations of the foregoing conversation. He avoids at all costs talking *about* creativity as if it is an object separate from the character. I emphasise this because it is more common for practitioners to talk about a matter than it is to enter the spirit of improvisation and talk from within the experience. No one is interested in objective truths in this exercise. It is, rather, a creative, playful experiment about creativity.

Invite Creativity to share reflections

The facilitator asks questions and invites Creativity's reflections from listening to the earlier interview. Creativity's thoughts, feelings, and associations are included. There is no strict code for organising the responses, simply to do so with good intentions. They are offered to be of further assistance to the presenter. The style of response will be unique but the intention is benign because everyone has creativity in his or her being. Here are some questions to invite comment from the character of Creativity:

- In listening to the conversation, how would you like to comment on how we have talked about you/your place in [the presenter]'s practice?
- What would you like to say about the way you are helpful, and the ways in which you are somehow restricted?
- How did it feel to be talked about in this way?
- What reflections do you have on your future part in [the presenter]'s repertoire of practice?
- What advice, if any, can you offer?

Open conversation between all three participants

The exercise is completed by the facilitator's returning to the presenter and inviting her responses to hearing Creativity talk about her, followed by a general discussion between all three participants to round off. Any specific learning points can be noted. Sometimes, the effect of the exercise is best mulled over later, rather than trying too soon to put words to the experience. Each person will have his or her own preferences, of course. For some, the exercise can be very moving.

The exercise is usually repeated to allow all participants to experience the different positions in relation to their creativity.

A tip is to change seats after each exercise, to assist in letting go the previous role.

Feedback from workshop participants suggests that this exercise, with its playful and performative dimensions, helps participants to loosen up their prejudices about creativity and perceived restrictions upon them as "possibilists".

It is variously described as "powerful", "moving", "energising", all words that illustrate the usefulness participants found in trying out something which helped focus on their relationship to creativity. At the same time, the exercise was itself an enactment of a creative process.

The other typical response to this exercise is a great sense of relief:

"It was good to find time and opportunity to talk with others about this important aspect of practice in a neutral space."

"It inspires me to keep going."

A range of responses added to our communal learning about what assists in maintaining creativity. Many proposals were similar to those described earlier by the Swedish colleagues:

- a desire for more open practice, more joint work;
- the need to reinstate time for self and other care;
- solidarity in developing proposals to alter restrictive practices;
- an approach to practice that celebrated creative initiatives;
- a decision to experiment more, and push one's practice repertoire.

Participants tuned into one another's creative potential and ability to enjoy their practice. Enjoyment had never been absent, but was sometimes slumbering, or tired by so many other "must do" activities that had stifled enjoyment.

This chapter has concentrated on the contexts that can promote creativity between practitioners and our clients; it has explored the various contexts in which creativity may thrive, both for the practitioner in her development of knowledge, its expression through her unique style, and in how a spirit of generosity can be maintained, informed by a systemic humanist orientation to practice.

Alongside the light of creative explorations is the shadow of constraints and this tension between the two domains is also expressed in the ways we listen and respond to one another. As a practitioner, my aim is to promote opportunities that arise in a therapy session that move beyond the stultifying effects of "the same damn thing time and time again". I try to recognise my expertise without shutting down the other, or permitting the other to close me down. Dialogue can be robust to be usefully creative.

At the micro-political level, the relationship between creativity and constraint is expressed in how we listen to one another, and how we try to respond in ways that are both humanising and co-creative, to expand our repertoire of possibilities without burying the constraints to vision. This is the focus of the next chapter, in which the micro-politics of how we listen and respond are in tension, and sometimes opposition, with macro-political influences pushing us from behind.

CHAPTER FOUR

Listening and responding: ethical practices and constraints

A central belief of systemic humanism is the creative potential of every human being to overcome oppressive contexts in their lives: in therapeutic and social practices, this entails challenging features that fail to try to transform human distress into human achievement. The practitioner actively contributes towards this goal, and, in so doing, both client and practitioner become participants in a process of mutual humanisation. The practitioner, like the client, is encouraged to challenge those ideas and ways of acting that constrain options for becoming other than they appear (Holzman, 2009). To do this, the practitioner looks towards therapeutic possibilities in direct work with the clients, as well as to a critique of organisational features and social–political forces that shape organisational procedures and policies. It is, wherever possible, a co-operative endeavour, but one that allows for debate and disagreement as well as consensus.

"It is in listening to the student that I learn to speak with him or her" (Freire, 1998, p. 106).

The way in which we listen and respond to another is an expression of such humanising principles. In this chapter, I set out some ways in which systemic humanism is expressed in our manner of listening and responding to our clients, and how they may listen and respond to us. In addition, I discuss constraints posed to humanising practices, and their detrimental influence on our ways of listening to the others we meet.

Our practice repertoire is always open to development. Forms of listening that have within them a generous spirit are ones that are geared to enhancing the potential of others in challenging their sense of oppression and enhancing their agency over their lives. Our job includes listening out for possible openings that connect us in a joint form of action. "We are not here trying to invent solidarity but to make ourselves conscious of it" (Gadamer, cited in Palmer, 2001, p. 35). We try to value the moment of meeting with another as a precious opportunity for change.

> In most . . . psychotherapies there is rush toward meaning leaving the present moment behind. We forget that there is a difference between meaning, in the sense of understanding enough to explain it, and experiencing something more and more deeply. (Stern, 2004, p. 140)

The general principles of attentive listening involve the ability to reflect in, and on, action (Schon, 1986), listening without immediate judgement, endeavouring to meet the client on equal terms as one human being to another while attending to our embodied responses, not just our immediate conceptualisation. Sensing how to judge an appropriate response, therefore, involves a critical appraisal of our reflections, holding back on the urge to "fix" a problem. These aspects of attentive listening are in "conversation", so to speak, with our prior experiences. We listen out for what seems to be called for in the immediate context. Openness to what is called for allows the practitioner to allow himself room for a degree of spontaneous responsiveness that fits the occasion. This is more adequately described as informed spontaneous responsiveness that is shaped by our noticing whether what we are saying is usefully fitting the occasion or failing to make a connection. It allows for immediate revision and improvisation. In our practice, sensitive listening and responding are core skills, necessary when we meet our clients, but there are several ways in which these aims can be tarnished or even thwarted.

Contextual features influencing how we listen and respond

An often-heard criticism of current demands on health service professionals is the squeezing out of the "reflective space"—a metaphor for the reflexive process of sensitive, therapeutic practice. To be "present in the moment" has almost reached the level of a cliché, but it is a very important phrase with which to deliberately remind ourselves that pausing for reflection, considering an appropriate response while attending to all our senses as sources of information, is crucial. While we are attentive to the details of connection "in the present moment", the systemic humanist practitioner keeps in mind the socio–political features that shape and inform the way in which we act and think "in the moment" as social beings.

We cannot separate our interaction with clients from the socio–political contexts that inform what it is possible to do. So, when we listen, we are doing this within a context that is also imbued with expectations about how and what we should do to meet the demands of our employing organisation. We cannot set our practice aside from the socio–political imperatives that help or hinder what we try to do. For this reason, listening and responding within a systemic humanising orientation demands a critical appraisal of the wider socio–political dimensions to our practice.

The reality of daily practice puts the textbook rules of attentive listening under pressure. Time-limited practice, curtailed by bureaucratic procedures, restricts the reflective space needed to make sensitive, useful responses. In addition, when models of practice seem to dictate procedures, creative human responsiveness suffers, and when members of staff are under insurmountable pressures, caring for one another also suffers.

> If no one cares when someone takes the trouble to do things right, nothing changes and the overwhelming message to the people who work at the front line . . . is that no one notices excellence and no one cares . . . That is the biggest source of burn out and discouragement for health care workers everywhere. (Gawande, 2014)

The organisational context of our practice also influences how we listen and respond and the ways we put listening into words. For example, objectifying language within the culture of an organisation will affect the way we think. Procedures and processes that demand categorical descriptions of people and their problems can influence by degrees the ways we think about what we are doing. If objectifying language takes hold as a dominant "dialect" in mental health, the practitioner can be willingly or unwittingly caught up in this form of discourse.

Language can bewitch

I am present at a case discussion at a CAMHS (Child and Adolescent Mental Health Team) multi-disciplinary meeting. The room is filled with colleagues from social work, psychiatry, and psychological therapies, including family therapy. We are all listening as a colleague presents the case of a child who is ten years old. The boy has been assessed by a psychologist who suggests that earlier assessments for autistic spectrum disorder (ASD) and attention deficit hyperactivity disorder (ADHD) might require further exploration. In addition, she comments that as the child tidied up at the end of the assessment session, he put all the toys precisely and meticulously back in place. Following this, she pondered whether the boy might also be showing symptoms of obsessive–compulsive disorder (OCD). I listened to the way this dedicated colleague focused attention only on the criteria for diagnosis, and on how the assembled team members listened attentively, nodding in support of her suggestions for further testing. The conversational parameters excluded any discussion of the relationship between the colleague and her client, or consideration of any other aspect of the child's life or his abilities.

I became increasingly concerned by the lack of curiosity from our present group and the colleague's absence of critical attention to her diagnostic formulations. I was also aware of feeling tense about raising questions within this largely compliant group. Each suggestion for further assessment of the boy was reinforced organisationally, since the CAMHS team had already established specialist services to assess ADHD and ASD in children. The child had now been considered a candidate for at least three mental health disorders but, as yet, we did not know his name.

Eventually, I enquired as to the boy's name, and asked the case presenter to imagine how he might reply if he were present and asked what service *he* might want from us. My colleague looked pensive, but did not know what the child would say. However, later she told me that the question had made her stop and think. The question had invited her to exercise her imagination, to make a guess. She told me of her extensive training; of how rich and stimulating her studies had been in exploring psychology and psychotherapeutic approaches. She emphatically praised her profession, and affirmed her wish to continually pursue creativity in her practice, but she also spoke of how her thinking had been dominated by the language of assessment, of working only within the diagnostic categories available to access treatment. Her independence of thought had been curtailed. The question about the boy's wishes had provoked her to consider the child's perspective, and possible concerns. This child-focused perspective had always been available to her but had become clouded by discourses that obscured more imaginative possibilities for her work. This does not simply argue against the potential usefulness of certain diagnostic formulations in specific circumstances. Instead, it argues *for* the value of rich debate and width of perspectives of which only one angle is to look for individual pathology.

This scene from practice raises questions about the ways in which we may struggle to maintain a humanising attitude to our clients, and to our colleagues.

It was not only that the colleague had offered a reductionist style of description of the child, but also that the contribution of the assembled group did not encourage a more systemic, humanising mode of enquiry. We benefit from a wide repertoire of responsivity to connect effectively with clients and contexts in which our humanity in practice excellence is acknowledged and encouraged; otherwise, as my colleague experienced, the life and soul of practice might wither. Freire sees a reductionist mentality as essentially anti-democratic:

> ... the reductionist mentality that talks only of training skills strengthens the authoritarian manner of speaking from the top down. In such a situation, speaking "with" which is part and parcel of any democratic vision of the world, is always absent, replaced by the more authoritarian form, speaking "to". (1998, p. 103)

Valuing doubt and uncertainty

The example also highlights the importance of colleagues in creating a context within which practitioners can express doubt and uncertainty and support each other in the complex endeavour of working in ways that can bring out the best in us. If our critical capacities are curtailed, we are likely to suffer and, more importantly, so are our clients.

One anxious practitioner told me with great conviction, "This client will not respond to individual counselling, as research shows that for her problem, group work is the most appropriate method."

This was said with such an air of certainty that it was difficult to offer another view. I soon learnt that the client in question had not wanted to continue to meet with the practitioner after the second session, but, instead of looking at the quality of the relationship between the two parties, the practitioner had resorted to presumed "scientifically proved" reasons not to continue with the young client. Like the rest of us, this practitioner was anxious to appear competent. He felt the need to present himself as knowledgeable to his senior colleagues but his desire to convey professional competence stopped short of entertaining uncertainty as a resource.

If I am determined to be seen as right, and defend my position against all odds, then listening is restricted. Resorting to scientific findings becomes less of a catch-all justification when we appreciate the unique and complex nature of working with people in distress. Specialist treatment models can make a useful contribution to practice when amended and made more flexible to fit the demands of complex practice.

Listening and responding benefits from an attitude of curious exploration of our reactions, including a tendency to rush towards certainty. Unless we feel safe enough to entertain and voice alternative views, rather than hide behind professional status or model "must dos", our range as practitioners will not develop. When confronted by procedures that feel punitive and impositional, it is difficult to speak up, even more so if one's position within an organisation is marginal, or where strict hierarchies of status operate as to whose opinions are to be given priority. The flow of conversation is blocked when the language of the powerful is denigrating, scoffing, overly assertive, or carries an air of certainty about it. In such situations, dialogue is silenced and, when this happens to me, I usually think again about how to present my views, and in what setting they might be better listened to.

I am reminded of a family session in which the grandfather looked at me with scepticism, as if the conversation with his family was really a waste of time. I tried not to be organised by his critical expression and dismissive behaviour towards me. At one point, I decided to explore his views on the idea of meeting as a family group and his apparent reservations about the usefulness of this way of working. When I did this, I felt less organised by his critical demeanour; I had found a little of the "wise fear" Socrates called courage. However, I was still nervous.

At the end of the session, he said, "I think you were very nervous." It was a great relief. I told him that he was right and that he had made a very astute observation. The ice was broken. In further sessions, he was more able to take part, and I was more able to relax a little and challenge him some more.

To admit to feeling nervous or unsure is sometimes considered a weakness, yet the admission of this is a natural feature of therapeutic endeavour. Our competence is conveyed by our more candid acceptance that feeling nervous and uncertain can be a point worthy of exploration; for example, we can ask of ourselves and others relationally focused questions exploring the theme of uncertainty from a position of curiosity about its relevance in supervision, or together at appropriate times with clients. Some examples could include the following.

- How come this situation is making you so uncertain?
- What are the feelings/behaviours that raise uncertainty in you?
- How do you begin to explain these to yourself?
- Who else in the context (clients/other practitioners/extended family, etc.) shares your uncertainty about how to go on?
- Why do you think this person holds a similar/different view?
- If uncertainty could be more of an ally in your practice, what could it tell you that would be useful to your clients?
- If your uncertainty were brought into direct discussion with the clients, who, if anyone, would feel relieved that you had brought this up?

These types of exploratory questions can begin to shift the theme of uncertainty from being an obstruction to practice towards a more curious engagement in practice. We need to be clear that when we openly discuss our insecurities and doubts, it is in the service of trying to be useful. All practice is a dance of intimacy; knowing how and when to address sensitive matters of vulnerability is, as ever, context dependent.

Modes of listening

There are two basic modes of listening: listening in order to speak, and speaking in order to listen (Hoffman, 2002, p. 247). The distinction between these two modes can help us to be clearer about the ways in which we might choose to respond in the ebb and flow of conversation. The pace and timing of our responses are in tune with the silence we leave between the spoken words. To listen in order to speak places the listener as accompanist, encouraging the speaker to open more thoughts and reflections on the words they hear themselves say. When our words come back to us, we can allow fresh understandings and feelings to be given attention.

The one who speaks to listen is saying, in effect, "After you!" When we are silently listening to another person, we can more readily "enter into the rhythm of the speaker's thought and experience that rhythm as language" (Freire, 1998, p. 104).

On the other hand, when listening in order to speak, I am more likely to be thinking ahead as to what I would like to put across to the other, perhaps a suggestion, perhaps a leading question to elicit information. In this mode, I am more actively leading the conversation and might have some end goal in mind, such as when we must make an investigative interview. When we lead the conversation too much, the client could feel constrained to comply with the direction we have set. This occurs typically in situations where, as practitioners, we are trying to instruct the other, but fail to listen sensitively to their responses, perhaps seeing the client as resistant, obstructive, or oppositional. Listening in order to speak can be extremely useful when the other is open and willing to hear what you must say; however, if taken to extreme, this mode can carry the weight of an authoritarian attitude that "presupposes that the listener's time is also the speaker's time" (Freire, 1998, p. 104). Busy practitioners with little time and too many assessments might fall prey to too much listening to speak, and we can rest assured that the recipients will know they are being talked *at*, not *with*.

In monological mode, we listen in order to speak, and although not all monologue is dehumanising, all dehumanising is monological. We try to convince the other to agree with our point of view without acknowledging dissent, except to argue against, or quash, it. This is a bid for "safe certainty" (Mason, 1993); it also applies when our clients come to us with definite opinions about what is wrong and how to fix it. A desire to achieve safe certainty is best responded to by trying to appreciate the strongly held opinion being proposed and its concomitant logic. We try to make sense of it, since the client is unlikely to be able to consider alternative views until his own have been offered some validation. However, if the position does not alter despite one's appreciative endeavour, then monologue prevails and dialogue is lost, at least for the time being. "A person who is not ready to put his or her prejudices in question is also someone to whom there is no point in talking" (Gadamer, in Palmer, 2001, p. 44).

There is nothing wrong in giving advice, only in failing to attend to the responses of the recipient of our suggestions. To try to impose a suggestion is arrogant when there is no consideration of how the listener might respond. Difficult emotional matters cannot be soothed away with easy solutions but it is tempting to put forward suggestions prematurely when faced with profound sadness and distress. Gawande addresses our natural temptation to dispense advice and treatment when, in fact, the patient (in this instance, patients with a terminal illness) would benefit more from care in the face of their inevitable demise, "Curbing our purely medical imperatives [and] resisting the urge to fiddle, fix and control" (Gawande, 2015, p. 149) when the outlook is bleak.

To be tentative with one's opinions can yield more in the way of co-operative exploration and joint action than making statements that seem to define the "truth" of the matter, and colonise the conversation.

The late Tom Andersen distinguishes three forms of listening and responding, according to different forms of reality presented to us; the first is the either/or reality, where definitions are made and remain fixed, irrespective of context. This would correspond to the world of inanimate objects: a stone is a stone is a stone. The second is the both/and reality, in which many simultaneous descriptions are possible in a context, but Andersen goes one step further and describes a third form of responsiveness in a neither/nor reality, in which we experience something taking place, "but we do not have an exact linguistic description for it" (Seikkula & Arnkil, 2014, p. 112). Stern (2004) addresses the failure of language to adequately encompass the indefinable quality of responsiveness:

> Change is based on lived experience. In and of itself verbally understanding, explaining or narrating something is not sufficient to bring about change . . . An event must be lived with feelings and actions taking place in real time, in the real world, with real people in a moment of presentness. (p. xiii)

This is an acknowledgement of the multi-sensorial complexity of listening and responding, and is a characteristic of a spirit of generosity in practice. When we are too busy thinking about what something means, or what we need to do next to complete our assessments, we might well miss the significance of what is also being "said" beyond words by our clients. All the non-verbal, paralinguistic, and performative contributions of language convey our general attitude towards the other. Do we look interested? Are we sitting too formally? Is our tone too sympathetic? Is our voice too quiet? We meet the other as a human being in the totality of our presence, in movement, gesture, and facial expression, all of which convey the nature of our invitation to the ones we meet. If our heads are down, and we are looking attentively at a list of questions on a piece of paper, then we are likely to convey to our clients that the questionnaire is more important than the person before us.

The generous listener will not impose specific directions on the client. It would not work if they did. Ultimately our clients will judge the "fit" and impact of what we do and say. Yet, in some organisational and practice contexts, the client who is not responding as the practitioner predicts is considered unmotivated, resistant, or in some way inadequate, unable to use the methods being applied to help. However, if practice is considered a process of humanisation, the onus is on the practitioner to search for ways to "fit" client preferences, styles, and needs, and discover ways to make the helping process jointly constructed between all participants, wherever possible.

If I think I have a good idea to share with my clients, I try to resist the temptation to blurt it out, especially if I am impressed with my apparent cleverness. In times like this I try (though do not always succeed) to hold back and wait; my bright idea has inspired me but there is no guarantee it will equally inspire the clients. My internal "editor" can help to digest, reshape, and choose the timing and expression of the idea. When we have done a thorough job of assessment, it is understandable if we are tempted to feel that our words carry the weight of authority and truth. We can be taken aback when the clients disagree. At such a juncture, it is prudent not to try to convince the client, but deal instead with their apparent disconnection with the formulation offered. This is an expression of systemic humility as a guard against "falling in love "with our own ideas.

At the same time, for dialogue to be useful, it also includes listening in order to challenge and debate.

Taking a risk to challenge

A woman, Simone, and her family had been coming to see me for family therapy for four sessions. Each time Simone and her three children came, she looked sad and defeated by life's struggles. She had been divorced for many years from a man who had been violent towards her and dominated her life. She was finding difficulty in raising her three sons and had little family support. It seemed she had no strength to change anything in her life. She saw herself as a victim who had lost hope. She found it very difficult to make decisions and had little energy for anything apart from daytime television. I had been trying to support her in finding some new direction in her life, but nothing I had said or done thus far had helped her to take a step forward.

My sympathetic listening and gentle suggestions masked my growing irritation that I was doing all the work to get the client moving. My ideas and suggestions were met with defeat and resignation. My questioning techniques produced no curiosity. While this impasse continued, I was also deeply concerned that the three children were becoming more distressed and showing increasing signs of troubling behaviours. Eventually, and with a degree of exasperation and concern, I said, "This isn't going to work, Simone. Meeting me is making no difference. The way we are talking just goes around in circles. There is more to you than this and it's time to make a move. We can't get anywhere just going over the same ground."

She looked alarmed and started to cry. I immediately thought I had challenged her too strongly and had completely undermined her already weak personal resources. However, at the same time I also felt freed and, instead of feeling irritated with Simone, I felt sympathetic and able to challenge her without feeling persecutory. My irritation was translated into words that seemed more useful in taking a step in our work together. This woke up both of us to a more robust manner of talking. It was more honest and direct. I had stopped treating the client like a delicate ornament that I worried about breaking; instead, my manner suggested she was strong enough to take a challenge without collapsing.

This example suggests a range of possible responses, rooted in a co-operative style of address that also permits robust challenges. It is premised on the belief that each person is imbued with creative power to begin to alter their circumstances. But, of course, this is a matter of co-creativity and joint action. I challenged the relational features of our interaction that were irritating me. It was the communicational circle of certainty that was problematic, not Simone. Even so, she clearly felt distressed at seeing my frustration, yet it did not escalate into her feeling abandoned (something that had been a pattern in her life); instead, we addressed the unproductive, complementary style of relationship to try something different.

Improvisation in ways of listening and responding

As practitioners, we need to be in tune to accompany our clients' words, actions, and emotional atmosphere, like an improvising musician. Each improvisation should play to the family's style of address, not completely, but sufficiently so that the meeting becomes a process of joint activity where differences of whatever kind find ways of being accepted rather than becoming barriers between our prejudices.

Playing to the family's "music"

A very noisy argument is heard in the waiting room as I am about to meet Jess, Olivia, Sarah, Pete, and Terry—five adults in conflict with each other. They enter the therapy room talking loudly to one another, shouting, joking, making large gestures, and all talking at once. I need to find a way to engage in a style that fits the "musical language" of the family. At one point, the jokes turn to me.

> "You're Scottish, aren't you? . . . like that comedian. What's his name?"
> "Billy Connolly", shouts the grandfather, Terry, and everybody laughs.

Now, there is no point in becoming straightfaced at this joke about me. In fact, the joke is an opening.

"Do you like Billy Connolly?" I say, and they nod.

"He learnt everything from me!"

This was met by general laughter and a lessening of tension. Right at the outset I am called upon to be the host conductor, and in later sessions I became less central as I learnt to follow their explorations about the painful events in their lives. Their boisterous humour and argumentative ways of interacting helped to bring them through times of deep distress. At first their "music" was lively, like a cabaret act, but as the practice progressed, the tone of the sessions became more serious, like a slow orchestral movement. The rhythm of conversation slowed, leaving more space to talk of painful matters in a useful way.

To accompany the client, as in family therapy, we might also be called upon to conduct the "music" in a more directive way to create some safe enough structure within which we can later improvise. Each family has its own style of interactional music; knowing how to accompany them is not so easy when there are many people in the "orchestra".

Loud "music" and a tender heart

I recall meeting a father and his son for a first session in a mental health service. The father, Mr Smith, was furious with the police for arresting his son, and furious with mental health and social care services for threatening to remove the boy to a psychiatric inpatient unit. The father clearly wanted to vent his anger at anybody associated with the mental health team, and I happened to be the consultant on duty who was in the firing line.

At one point, the father said to me, "Frankly, I don't give a fuck about you!" (pointing a finger, pistol-style at me). "And I don't give a fuck about you either" (similarly gesturing towards my colleague). "All I give a fuck about is him! " (pointing to his embarrassed, fifteen-year-old son).

I said, "*That* is the main thing, Mr Smith."

There was something overly dramatic in his performance of finger pointing, and in the way he swore about caring for his son; at the same time, I felt an odd, almost light-hearted response to him. It was something to do with the juxtaposition of care and cursing that made me think this man was desperate for help and this was his way of showing it. People have different ways of expressing their strength of feeling for one another. He did it in front of us by swearing his concern for his son. I also thought at the time his actions were like the nip that denotes the bite. There was an element of play fighting about Mr Smith's manner.

This was the start of a bumpy series of loud and challenging family therapy sessions but, at baseline, we were all meeting because the family wanted to improve matters for their son. Listening for possibilities to make a useful connection can bolster creative connections with clients even when they "invite" us into a battle with them.

I emphasise this here because practitioners caught in the headlamps of scrutiny can become rigid in trying to follow a protocol instead of following feedback. This error is compounded in organisations that, perhaps for understandable reasons, have become risk averse. In the above example, it might have paid off to say to Mr Smith that we would not tolerate foul language expressed in a threatening fashion. Maybe he would have complied. That is always a possibility. But Mr Smith had already been in frustrated, angry exchanges with police and duty social workers, so there was a fair chance he would have immediately charged us with the same critical attitude towards him.

Sometimes, of course, it is necessary to invoke rules about threatening behaviour, especially where personal safety is at risk. However, in Mr Smith's case, the risk would have escalated had we become critical and admonished him for swearing; instead, the context was more open to alternatives because of the *way* we listened to his accusations. His finger pointing stood for a fight but it was not the same as a real fight.

Knoblauch (2000) proposes a model of resonant minding which is concerned with unfolding relational processes that I consider to be essential in any approach to humanising practices. The particularity of his model of resonant minding has its focus on an action or feeling as part of an unfolding process, always moving no matter how stable a relationship or context seems to be. Responsiveness to feelings is centrally important, "Just as improvising jazz soloists and accompanists recognise and respond to displays of nonverbal dimensions of tone rhythm and harmony" (p. 96). This is not an impulsive responsiveness but to be "absorbed in a continual process of reflection and reconsideration, to be introspective and empathic, to make choices deriving meaning from the relational context" (p. 97). Knoblauch, thus, focuses on the two-person relationship between analyst and analysand, but the idea of resonant minding has its place in wider contexts, such as in family work and couple therapy. Here, the musical complexity could be wider in scope, more like a quartet or small orchestra than a duet, but the principal of resonant responsiveness can still be useful.

Listening to our prejudices[1]

Improvisation in therapeutic practice is a type of informed spontaneity that is context related and within which constraints and possibilities emerge in the unfolding process of meeting another.

This sets up a challenge for practitioners to focus critically on our own prejudices or strongly held beliefs about what needs to be done (Cecchin et al., 1994). We all hold prejudices. The challenge is to try to hold them with an eye on their power to blind us to alternative views. Even when we feel we are not at the mercy of prejudices, they can wake from their sleep to alert us to their potency.

As a Protestant who grew up in Glasgow with Belfast working-class parents, I learnt at an early age to hate Catholics just because they were Catholics. As I grew up, I actively opposed this sectarian prejudice and put it to sleep—or so I thought. Many years later, I took a walk with my close friend Gerry Cunningham, a Catholic from Belfast, on the other side of the "Peace Line" from my family of origin. We took a stroll along the Falls Road, marked by statues of the Virgin Mary and pavements coloured in the green, white, and gold of the Republic. I quickly felt uneasy, but when we then walked across to the Shankhill Road, with the Union Jack flying above the shop fronts and kerbstones painted the red, white, and blue of Unionism, I felt immediately "at home". My friend had the same reaction in reverse. The cues of sectarianism in the colours and symbols created a reaction of insecurity or tribal belonging that was embedded in our respective histories and, equally, embodied in our reactions. The difference was that now we could talk of the presence of prejudice without it organising our responses to one another. In fact, our resultant conversation seemed to bond our friendship even more.

In my practice as a psychotherapist, my anti-diagnostic prejudice about ADHD (Wilson, 2013), is very firmly rooted, but I also need to recognise that for some parents a belief in drug treatment for their child is held with an equally strong conviction, so I need to suspend the expression of my conviction, at least for a while, to see what is possible. In other words, I must try to hold fast to my view that the parents have the right to explore the biomedical treatment of their child. In discussion, when the time is right, I also allow myself to discuss the possible side effects and the wider concerns that have an impact on the child's mental health. However, in the end, I allow my prejudice to have its say without denigrating the parents for their viewpoint. I offer my reservations without trying to convince the parents that they are wrong. However, I do try to create a more relational view of their child's problem. I am a systemic therapist and this is one prejudice I find generally very useful.

Irreverent listening and responding: necessary but insufficient

Cecchin and colleagues (1992) suggest that to respond to the constraints of an institution, a practitioner needs to be armed with an attitude of irreverence towards any prescribed ways of working. This attitude is intended to help free the practitioner from feeling trapped by predictable behaviours, methods, and ways of thinking that would constrain her freedom to act. Cecchin points to the challenge of therapists who feel imprisoned by their professional identity and try to avoid this. In order not to be imprisoned by predictability, Cecchin decided always to do something different; he points out that this position also poses an identity problem, as being unpredictable can itself become predictable. A healthy dose of irreverence is, indeed, important to avoid being "boxed in" as a practitioner. The added dimension within systemic humanism is to broaden the realm of irreverence to include an active critique of dehumanising organisational and professional constraints, and to promote anti-oppressive practices on behalf of clients and colleagues. Irreverence in this context is, therefore, also political in its practice.

Keeney (1992), in his Foreword to *Irreverence: A Strategy for Therapists Survival* (Cecchin et al., 1992), provides an account of The Feast of Fools as a symbolic representation of irreverence in a different context from therapy. The festival acts to temporarily reverse the usual societal hierarchies, but once the impudent feast is over, the status quo reasserts itself. In this sense, the irreverent performance of the peasants and the landed gentry in effect serves only to re-establish the current political and hierarchical regime. So, while an irreverent attitude might provide a useful form of survival strategy, in Freire's terms, this is a domesticated form of practice.

Alternatively, irreverence within systemic humanism proposes the ideal of transforming oppressive practices and the political interests that support them. It is not the irreverence of the festival that matters so much as the active participation in refusing to return to the status quo.

Although Cecchin's concept does not directly address this wider contextual influence, the qualities of irreverence encourage practitioners to step beyond any orthodoxy as to how to behave as a therapist and, instead, entertain creative doubts about any one approach to therapy providing all the answers. The radical, irreverent therapist refuses to follow obligatory steps for therapy procedures or protocols where he thinks they are counterproductive. This attitude stands in opposition to those claims by advocates of models of practice that rely on practitioners' compliance with procedures stipulated by the model. Each step is followed religiously, and each practitioner is schooled in the model through supervisors who direct action, often at a great distance from the particularities of each client–practitioner relationship.

There are many ways of construing and responding to a situation. The main purpose is to find a construction that is most useful to therapeutic progress. Listening irreverently picks up on possibilities for new ways of challenging old ways of thinking and doing. This applies as much to the therapist as it does to the clients. Irreverent listening and responding create conditions in which something new can emerge. The push is towards creating useful differences, not definitive explanations, except, of course, when explanations lead to useful new directions. Irreverence, here, is allied to Fromm's ideas on dissidence that include a refusal to say what we do not see as relevant to effective practice.

Reverence towards the status quo limits creative practice

Some years ago, I was presenting a workshop to a group of psychologists in a rather tightly organised institution for child mental health.

I showed a clip from practice of two young boys playing on the floor creating a mini sculpture of their lives in foster care (Wilson, 1998). I was lying on the floor beside them, asking questions about the story as it unfolded. Later, a practitioner took me aside to tell me that he would not be allowed to behave in such a playful, informal way, as it was not considered proper professional demeanour.

To remain flexible in one's ways of working can be a daunting prospect, and raises questions about the dominant culture of any institution, and the degree to which one's professional autonomy is curtailed by ideas about remaining reverential towards expected norms for one's professional activities.

The overly compliant practitioner, holding organisational views with too much reverence, will adhere to the given conditions of practice even when they offend his own ethical stance. Take, for example, the practitioner who knows that drugs are being too readily prescribed for children who have been given a diagnosis of ADHD. To comply with the dominant professional language of biomedicine, the reverent practitioner will rationalise his decision to go along with the over prescribing. This practitioner's argument might run as follows: "By getting the ADHD diagnosis the family gain access to more social welfare benefits, and better acceptance of the child's behaviour in school". The apparently reverential practitioner might also hide his criticisms through fear of being marked out as a maverick. Yet, the costs can be very high to those who appear reverent towards ideas they do not believe in. Contradictions between what one strongly believes (our prejudices) and how one behaves can mean that there is no choice but to practise in ways that offend one's professional ethics and personal values. When we are hemmed in by protocols that limit the expression of our repertoire as practitioners, we can become disillusioned. On the other hand, "When the therapist believes that the treatment is efficacious, he or she will enthusiastically communicate that belief to the client" (Wampold, 2011, p.183). The strength of enthusiasm for a contextual approach does not in itself make for a successful outcome, but this finding confirms the centrality of hope and commitment as crucial components of an effective alliance between practitioner and client.

Too much reverence towards imposed methods and structures for practice places restrictions upon ways of assisting our clients that could be more effective; it restricts professional autonomy and passion in carrying out our clinical work.

It is part of our professional duty to address questions that challenge ideas that we consider to be detrimental to the clients. "Whistleblowing" is supported by many organisations, in theory. In practice, the reality remains very different. Bullying, professional ostracism, and protracted legal proceedings come at a severe cost to those who point the finger at malpractice. To challenge the Emperor about his new clothes is courageous but can be very costly. This response falls under the category of "Whatever you say ... say nothing", a term coined by the late poet Seamus Heaney when describing the silencing of dissent in the face of sectarian threat during "The Troubles" in Northern Ireland.

At a group case discussion in one setting, I was asked to offer my ideas on the effect of changes to procedures leading to more bureaucratic form-filling and goal-setting. I expressed my view that the form-filling and goal-setting seemed largely to ignore the very important matter of how our young clients viewed the service we were trying to deliver. I remarked that typical responses from young clients and their families emphasised the value of meeting with a practitioner on whom they could depend, and as someone who would help them through the rough times. They did not often say much about the model or approach used by practitioners; rather, the feedback was reassuringly obvious: feeling understood, being listened to, being given advice and support by a practitioner who is friendly but not a friend, being helped to see things differently without taking sides. Our clients tell us, time and time again, how important it is to feel listened to and connected with.

To my surprise the response from some of my colleagues was of the need to comply, not rock the boat, and to stop discussing such "philosophical ideas"; if the institution requires assessments, goal-setting questionnaires, and models of work to be prescribed, then this is what must be done.

One colleague remarked that he would comply with all the "must dos" because he needed to hold on to his job to pay the household bills. He makes an important point. Yet, at the same time, I wondered about the costs of compliance. These comments sounded dispiriting to me. One worrying trend when job security is uncertain is the tendency for practitioners to create a self-protective wall between their specialism and other disciplines. Competition for scarce resources can create a worry that one's profession will suffer if resources go elsewhere. If we do not elbow potential rivals out of the way, goes the argument, maybe we will be the ones to lose out.

In one group exercise in advance of a retendering process, a mental health team was asked by senior managers to describe each discipline's capacities, specialisms, expertise, and so on to the whole staff group. Each profession was allocated some minutes to inform the assembled staff of the skills and range of client problems their discipline could successfully deal with. As I observed this performance, I noticed that each discipline seemed to be covering *all* the requisite skills needed to provide a comprehensive service to all comers in the service. The whole performance had an air of farce about it. The presenters looked awkward about (over) selling their wares. Rather than enhancing mutual appreciation of each profession's range of expertise, the exercise had a divisive effect.

"They think they can do everything!" was the often-whispered response. "We studied for years to get where we are and they think they can do it without the need to train properly . . . Everybody can do short term work . . . so, what's so special about their claim?"

Until this exercise in "promotional selling" (shown in the way each profession felt compelled to justify their relevance), the culture of the team had been openly collaborative and healthily competitive. Now each profession was being asked to display examples of expertise with a price tag (claims for short-term, evidence-based therapies were called upon; claims that the approach could easily be stretched to address a wide range of contexts of therapy—cognitive behavioural therapy (CBT) with families, psychotherapy with parents, family therapy and CBT combined in individual treatments, and so on). If each profession could argue the case to be able to meet all the various demands on the service, then what was the point of having separate disciplines at all? The underlying worry was that such competitive "tendering" (and there is nothing tender about it) would eat away at collaborative team relationships and replace them with a kind of professional *machismo* as to whose discipline had the biggest claim to effectiveness across the board. When the emphasis is on rivalrous promotion of a model or discipline, the fabric of team support unravels.

Fortunately, this tendency was discussed between staff in more informal conversations, and to some extent the worst competitive excesses of jockeying for the position of front runner were lessened.

Practitioners can choose to comply with a regime of treatment whose validity they might doubt but nevertheless feel compelled to support for reasons identified above. When I published a critical analysis of the biomedical model of ADHD, several colleagues expressed concern that my criticism would get me into trouble within the NHS service that employed me at the time. This did not happen, but I took their concern as a measure of caution experienced by colleagues about the danger of stepping out of line. It was not realised, but their fear that it *might* result in criticism or censure was what *did* worry me on behalf of my colleagues.

One colleague created a humorous cartoon lampooning the growing mountain of administrative procedures being introduced for recording "must dos". Someone suggested posting the cartoon on the notice board but, after discussion, this was thought to be a risky move as it might offend senior staff members who are responsible for implementing the new admininstrative procedures. The cartoon was eventually placed out of sight on the side of a filing cabinet.

This small episode illustrates the ways in which certain forms of irreverence can be frowned upon. Having a laugh at the expense of new procedures might be construed as disloyalty. If you are also concerned about whether your contract will be renewed, you might worry that this could go against you at your next review meeting. However, when humour and irony are lost to conversation, it is a major restriction on freedom to express criticism, even in satirical form. In a much wider context, colleagues from the Czech Republic who had grown up under the repressive communist regime described to me how humour helped them through. Hope for change was bolstered by being able to joke about, and satirise, the political regime that oppressed them. While this was kept under wraps, it was a necessary lifeline to their creative dissidence and opposition.

Catching up with you

I have considered the nuanced details of listening and responding, and have placed these within the possibilities and constraints open to us. By considering the contextual features influencing how we listen and respond, we become more aware of the ways in which organisational language informs this process, and how organisational language is, in turn, influenced by powerful policies on how to define and treat human distress. We are, therefore, always on the lookout for ethical challenges to effective practice posed by constraints that have an impact on our ability to respond with curiosity, irreverence, and a generous spirit. This also entails attention to our own prejudices, and our ability to attend to our critical consciousness. Listening and responding are ethical and political choices as to how we are affected by, and act upon, constraints placed upon us and our clients. This brings us back to doing what is possible to maintain our creative capabilities with our clients.

There is no ideal practice setting. Each organisation will have time limits, protocols, administrative procedures, and other "must dos", and not all constraints are anti-therapeutic. Perhaps you might like to pause here to consider those conditions in your own practice that are conducive to effective listening and responding and, equally, those that inhibit your creativity.

The "Why is this so?" exercise

- What contextual features (policies, pressures, team dynamics . . . aid or hinder your ability to respond creatively to your clients, and why is this so?
- What is the dominant style of language within your organisation that shapes the way clients are discussed and listened to, and why is this so?
- What perspectives are more marginalised in case discussions, and why is this so?
- What do you think your colleagues and your clients would say are your strengths as a listener/responder, and what does this tell you about your style and spirit as a practitioner?
- In responding to unhelpful constraints or practices which perturb you ethically, what steps are open to you to address these? Where are the strengths in your team to find support for such challenges?
- What, if anything, might tempt you to avoid raising your concerns, and why is this so?
- When do your prejudices about work with others aid your creativity, and in what circumstances do they seem to limit

creative listening and responding? Why do you think these prejudices feature in your practice?

To listen and respond is not only dependent on the quality of the meeting between individuals. Co-creativity requires a safe enough context to allow experimentation, promote imagination, and encourage irreverence in the joint search for therapeutic possibilities. The practitioner's place is to contribute her creativity and set the scene to enrich the creativity of the clients seeking help. It is essentially an improvisational process and, like any improvisation, it requires rigorous study and dedicated practice to feel free enough to try something different. The chapter that follows focuses on these important themes to enhance each practitioner's repertoire in supervision, teamwork, and therapy.

CHAPTER FIVE

Co-creative supervision and practice: experiment, improvise, and perform

How might practice be enhanced by creating opportunities for greater experimentation? The examples set out here are drawn from my experience of working in the National Health Services in the UK, and had to be negotiated within the strictures of limited time availability and waiting list demands. However, creating space and time to experiment paid dividends in keeping up our morale, mutuality of respect between team colleagues, and energy in trying to "recognise ourselves in the jobs we do". There is no shortcut to creativity in practice. I hope you find the examples useful in both supervision and in direct practice with your clients/patients. I also hope that you will see this chapter as a further expression of building practice upon the foundational ideas of systemic humanism and creativity discussed earlier. Here, we can explore together how our practice can push beyond the constraints we typically work under, while keeping an eye on doing what is possible.

Co-creativity as the expression of aesthetic practices

The educationalist Sir Ken Robinson (2001) makes the distinction between anaesthetic and aesthetic forms of education. Anaesthesia in education is characterised by linear, mechanistic forms of teaching; it is an industrial metaphor of education. Conformity, uniformity, and routine activities are promoted, and expertise is held within a hierarchically organised system. Standardisation is the aim, and it has the effect of sending spontaneity to sleep. His argument is that this industrial model of education is not relevant for today's children. It is outmoded and does not prepare them for twenty-first century life.

In contrast, aesthetic educational practices draw on an "organic" metaphor that promotes diversity in thinking, encourages experimentation, and the exercise of the imagination. It is a model of education with direct relevance in social care and mental health. It points towards the need to celebrate multiplicity of contributions in assisting clients, rather than being tied to only one way of proceeding.

One's freedom to experiment is influenced by the time available to think, opportunities to discuss ideas with colleagues and clients, and the support of our agencies to feel secure enough to improvise. The experimentalist practitioner is aware of both contextual and theoretical necessities in gauging what experiments are possible within any setting. I emphasise the aesthetic, experimental forms of co-creative practice as a way of placing practice within a systemic humanistic orientation. This orientation is not anti-science, but anti-scientism. Stierlin, in discussing family therapy as a science or an art form, proposes that practitioners should trust their artistic intuition with the conviction that

> in so doing we are also assisting the creative unconscious of our patients and families to find better solutions for themselves in their situations, solutions that might turn out completely different from anything we could possibly have imagined. And yet, despite, and perhaps even because of, the trust we place in the power of artistic intuition, the artistic unconscious, I also see a place, or rather an imperative necessity, in our work, for conceptual clarity, for discriminating reflection on the consequences of our therapeutic activity, for the constant formulation of falsifiable hypotheses. (Stierlin, 1983, p. 419)

For aesthetic experimentation to be useful, it should be lodged in ethical practice, with the clients' concerns as central to the aim of any coming activity. In effect, experimentation occurs when all parties feel the risk is worth taking because there is a hope, even anticipation, that the coming experiment will be useful, even if we are not sure about how.

In the following illustrations, the first addresses creativity in the context of the practitioner's tiredness, and the exercise of the imagination.

Practitioner as serious playmate

It is a Friday afternoon and it has been a long week. I am tired and looking forward to a relaxing evening meal and a good glass of wine. I have promised to visit a young client at his home. The father asked me to see his son on his own at the child's request. We have had a few family therapy sessions in my psychology department, but the boy, Alan, aged ten, has told his father that he does not like coming to the hospital. Consequently, Alan has asked his father if I could make a home visit, for a change. I arrive at the family home to be greeted by an anxious-looking father who says, "Hello Jim, Alan is in the sitting room waiting for you." He tells his son I have arrived, and then makes his exit "I'm just going upstairs for a shower."

I enter the living room and say hello to Alan. He is sitting on a large sofa at the other end of the room. I sit across from him, but the distance seems too far. He is about twenty feet away from me. I notice the thick pile of the fitted carpet; it looks very comfortable. I say, "Your dad said it would be OK for us to meet today." Alan nods.

"How's school?" I ask.
"Oh, OK ", he says, "but I'm not very good at maths." (Pause).
I say, "No—me neither." (Pause).
Alan says, "I can't do long division."
I hesitate, then say, "Have you got a pencil and paper?" He reaches for some paper.
"Would you mind if I came over to sit beside you?"
"No", he says, shrugging his shoulders. We then sit side by side as we struggle to figure out the best way to tackle his problem with long division.

Let me pause a moment. As I sit beside Alan, I recall a story told to me by a young psychiatrist. He recounted that once he was struggling to make a useful alliance with a young man who had recently had a psychotic episode. The young psychiatrist had offered to talk with his patient, after discharge home, about the possible effects of taking antipsychotic medication. However, clinic appointments offered to the patient had been missed. In desperation, the young psychiatrist made a visit to the patient's home, but the young client, though present in the meeting, had refused to get involved in the conversation that took place. The psychiatrist told me that while he was waiting for all the family members to assemble in the sitting room, the patient's younger brother was doing his maths homework, and was clearly struggling with it. So, the young psychiatrist offered to help, since he was good at maths.

The meeting ended with the young psychiatrist offering to see his patient the following week in the clinic. This time the young man turned up. The psychiatrist was intrigued as to why he had come this time, and asked his patient, who told him, "I could see how you helped my brother and so I thought, maybe, you can also help me."

Now, in the time it has taken you, my companion, to read this story, I imagine many associations and other random thoughts might have played on your mind. When we recall an incident like this one it comes in a flash, a momentary finger-snap of connection between two contexts, the psychiatrist's story and my experience in the room with Alan. When we recount the story in print, it unfolds in a different time frame.

This recollection came to me as I sat with Alan doing his maths.

To proceed,

> I say, "Your dad said it would be OK for us to discuss anything that might be worrying you." He nods. "Is there something that you would also like to discuss—you know—like the maths . . .?"
>
> Alan says that he cannot sleep at night because he keeps thinking that his right hand will come up and chop at his throat until he dies. He shows me the gesture and I repeat it so I know exactly the movement that he fears. I do not have any creative question to ask. I feel a bit stumped. I ask what he then does, and Alan tells me that he goes to his father's bedroom to say why he can't sleep. His father reassures him that this won't happen, and he goes back to his room.
>
> "Does that help you?" I ask.
>
> "No. I still lie there thinking my hand will chop at my neck," Alan replies.
>
> He is looking very unhappy at this point but I am not at all sure where to go next in the discussion. The carpet is inviting and I am tired. I say,

"Alan, would it be OK if I sat on the floor here?" He nods his consent and I sit down, leaning against the sofa. I ask him,

"So, you are lying in bed and your arm comes up like this?" (I repeat the gesture.) He nods, and then I decide to lie back on the carpet; as I do I close my eyes. Now I am flat on my back on the carpet. I am improvising. I say, with my eyes closed,

"So, you are lying in bed like this, and you think any moment your hand will strike at your throat like this?" I illustrate the gesture. With my eyes closed, I hear Alan say with some enthusiasm, "That's it!"

So, as I lie there, I continue, "... suppose there was a machine that you could invent that would somehow stop this hand from chopping ... What colour would it be?"

Immediately, Alan says, "Purple." And at that moment my fatigue vanished. I was inspired by the boy's willingness to enter this imaginative play with me.

This is a particularly vivid example of co-creativity to whet the appetite, but creativity occurs through the smallest of exchanges that can ultimately lead to problems being dealt with. The idea is to aim for creativity in context, in whatever small or more dramatic form it might take.

Reflection on practitioner as serious playmate

As I have already proposed, style is unique and not every practitioner will want to get down on the floor. What matters here is our ability to experiment and free ourselves a little from the professional and personal constraints that seem to limit modes of connection with clients. The tiredness I felt was jettisoned as soon as the boy answered my question about the colour of the machine. He entered the playground of practice (Wilson, 2007) where a context for serious play is created between participants. His creative response set the stage for the next step. Clearly, there is an element of theatre, drama, and apparent irreverence in this illustration. Colleagues have asked me, "What would the father have thought at seeing you lying on the floor chopping at your neck? Were you embarrassed at the prospect of being discovered by the father?" In fact, I was not particularly worried should the father return. He and I had sufficient mutual respect that I felt sure he would not have been anything other than mildly amused. The key point here is that the context felt safe enough to improvise and this sense of safety was created between us, leading up to the visit to see Alan at home.

The following example illustrates a further mode of performative practice that helps to open conversation on unexpressed matters of importance.

Practitioner as therapeutic go-between

I am meeting with a father, Nadir, and his son, Adem. We have already met for two sessions following Adem's referral to our mental health service because of his depression. He is a large, overweight seventeen-year-old who seems to have retired from the world. He spends his time nocturnally playing computer games. I learn that he is especially skilled in this arena, has many virtual contacts, and makes money by winning gaming competitions.

He is very low in mood when we meet. He finds it difficult to open discussion with his father. He seems shy and awkward when his father tries to tell him how much he should accept his help. However, Adem does not look convinced. The atmosphere at the beginning of this session has an air of expectation and desperation in equal measure.

At a certain moment, Nadir says, "I have always been a private man. I came to England as a child and no one helped me to speak English. My father was a drunk and nobody helped me until I had a really good teacher, Mrs Smith, who helped me to learn English."

Nadir started to become tearful and the more he opened up, the more Adem looked awkward and unsure about what to say or do. I decided to speak directly to Nadir and let Adem sit to one side for a while.

Nadir told me in detail about his isolation as a Turkish man who has no friends and had a very bad gambling problem until a year ago. He still gambles, but is trying to reduce the amount he spends.

"The men in the bookmaker's talk with me about betting, but once outside the betting shop I have no friendships. I am trying to help myself."

All this time I can see that Adem is not impressed. I think perhaps he has heard these claims to change from his father many times. Both father and son look sad and out of touch with each other except through their isolation. I feel that I am invited to become a bridge between them.

Now the challenge here, as always, is to find a way that is both supportive of the clients yet leaves room for trying to introduce a not too unusual difference.

Nadir looks to me, "I can't find the things to say to convince my son I mean it this time. Maybe if I can help him, he can also help me."

I take this as my cue to proffer an experiment, and ask if they would allow me to try something to find some words to offer to Adem. Nadir anxiously agrees. Adem looks a bit doubtful, but nods his tacit consent.

I ask them if I could say some words to express what I imagine Nadir harbours for his son but finds difficult to say himself. I explain that this would be something of an attempt that would require them both, later, to comment on my "guesswork", including telling me where I got it all wrong. It would need Nadir to critique my experiment, as no one can read another person's mind.

The room is quiet and I am sitting close to Nadir and across the table from Adem.

> "OK", I say, "Let me try to say some words to you, Adem, that may *also* be in the words and feelings your father wants to say but isn't able to do, so far."
>
> I look directly towards Adem and improvise. I find myself saying (recounted here in summary), "When I left Turkey as a child I didn't know anyone until I met Mrs Smith, my teacher, who helped me to learn English. I felt very lonely. My father didn't care much so I was left to bring myself up. I don't want you to be left out like I was. I want you to believe that I am trying very hard to stop gambling, but I know that is a lot to ask because I have said these things before. I have felt so lonely here in England, and you have your life ahead of you. I don't want you to waste it like I've done."
>
> At this point, I can see Nadir is tearful; I notice that as I speak I am also feeling heavy with sadness. I sigh as I come to the end of my rendition and we all sit in silence for a few moments. The father nods to me and I nod back; something crosses between us, as fathers, without words.
>
> I ask Adem if he wishes to comment on my experiment. The father listens as Adem tells me that he is very cautious about trusting his father to do the things he says he wants to do to help him. Nadir accepts this and tells me that my experiment was true to his feelings.

The atmosphere remains intimate between the three of us, and after a while the father and son begin to talk about what they plan to do—visit a relative in another part of England, go fishing . . .

The therapy also involved Adem's mother, who was intrigued at what happened when we three men met together, as she noticed a change in her husband and son following the sessions.

Reflection on practitioner as therapeutic go-between

Now, to consider this experiment from a systemic humanising approach is to emphasise the creative potential in father and son, as well as the practitioner, to jointly take a creative risk and experiment. The context was safe enough to do so. The experiment of offering to give words to the father's so far unexpressed feelings was couched in terms that both supported his desire for change and set out the challenge that such a desire needs to be put into action. The relational frame was in my mind particularly when I looked at Adem and saw his shy caution and response to my words. He looked as if he wanted to believe his father but was frightened to invest his hope once more.

This feedback shaped my response. I erred on the side of caution as I saw the cautious response from the young man. I caught the eye of the father as he looked increasingly moved by my words. In turn, I sensed the sadness in my own expressions and in my sigh (an internal signal to me that I needed to pause and let feelings settle).

As a systemic therapist, I could describe what I did as an attempt to create a generative dialogue; I was touching on the "not yet said" (after Anderson, 1997). I was cognisant of the relational process, and looking for options to find new possible directions for the father and son; I was also attempting to attend to my embodied responses, not just my intellectual processing of the father–son interaction and "isomorphic pattern" between them. The experiment of inner talk allowed all three of us an opportunity to become observers of our own processes; the promotion of observer perspectives and fresh experience emerged when each party was invested in this systemically orientated performance of practice. Some practitioners might see links with aspects such as mentalization processes (Verheugt-Pleiter et al., 2008). This can be a useful connection to help practitioners identify with elements of the improvisation. The emphasis placed here is on a systemic humanist *attitude* towards the contexts of co-creativity that attempts to tap into the creative power of each participant. The improvisation is useful only if it fits what the context calls for. Each small move seemed woven into the next one and connected to the preceding tiny steps in the exchanges between us all. The main matter at hand is to make sure the connection with the clients is rooted in a systemic humanising orientation in which techniques from whichever source may be welcomed.

Reflecting processes as playback therapy

A story of its beginning: my father, Hugh, used to tell me this story from his childhood: "When I was about five years old, I was playing under the kitchen table when my mother and aunt came in. They couldn't see me because the table cover hid me from them. I listened to their talk. At one moment, my aunt said to my mother, "Nothing good will become of Hugh" . . . And my mother didn't say anything. That has stuck in my mind."

My father recounted this story at times in his life when he would ruminate on lost opportunities of improving himself. He criticised himself for playing safe. It was saddening to hear him tell me the story of himself as a small boy, affected by criticism that went unchallenged by his mother. It was as if the story resided inside him, and surfaced whenever he had doubts about the merits of his life. In many other ways, he was a creative and well respected man, but this story acted like a weight that could not be put down. Somehow, the import of the story also resided within me, acting as a salutary lesson *not* to avoid opportunities that might present themselves in life. At the same time, the story saddened me when I thought of my father's disappointment in feeling that he had led too safe a life.

Then, one evening, I was invited by a colleague and family therapist, Kerri Newness, to attend a session of Playback Theatre. This was a revelation.

Playback Theatre is a form of creative, improvisational theatre, developed from psychodrama and the influences of Freire and Moreno in the 1970s, in which audience participation provides the stories, vignettes, or scenes from life for the acting company to perform. To describe the format briefly: a member of the audience is invited to tell a story to the actors which is then "played back" with nuanced artistic emphases, often using metaphorical language, music, and movement. In this way, a narrative is transformed into a portrayal of a situation that offers the story teller and audience an opportunity not only to revisit the story, but also to witness the portrayal offered, allowing for a fresh way of seeing and re-experiencing the story. It is a variation on reflecting processes, but one that is more actively dramatic and involves movement and dramatic device.

I decided to offer my father's story to the actors, acknowledging that it also affected me with certain feelings of regret on his behalf.

After recounting the story to the actors, I watched the portrayal, which was carried out with great sensitivity and respect, and felt enriched by new and different emphases placed on the tale I had recounted. The actor's characterisation of sadness had a touch of self-pity; regret was tinged with acceptance; the kitchen table had a life of its own and moved around! The portrayal of me, the son, joined in from time to time, asking questions from the side of the stage. What made the greatest impact on me was the realisation that *I was not the central character*; rather, I had only a bit part in this portrayal. As I watched, I became aware, for the first time, of how I had allowed the story to occupy a central part of feeling (unduly) sad on behalf of my father. The realisation that I was a minor character in the portrayal brought this home to me in an instant. Now portrayed in such an illuminating way, it held less sway over me. The weightiness of sadness and regret lifted. I could see the story for the first time in a new, light-hearted way. It did not have the same organising influence on my thoughts. In fact, the story itself took on new dimensions, including here as a resource to help convey, in print, the relationship between creativity and risk taking as a practitioner.

This episode gave me the idea of playback practices in therapy training and supervision (Wilson, 2015). The creativity of all participants is central to the modes offered in the following examples to develop fresh and useful dialogue in the way participants see and experience their lives, just as the portrayal of the story I told benefited me.

If you have tried the group exercise on creativity outlined in Chapter Three, I imagine you may have experienced already how such modes can open new possibilities to see matters differently. If not, perhaps this is an opportunity to get together with some colleagues and experiment.

Playback therapy team work with a family: my quandary

In a pre-therapy session, I am meeting with my colleagues about my sense of not getting very far with a father and son we are about to see. The father, Richard, wants help with his depressed son, Paul, and his son complains that his father should "get a life!" In other words, the son is worried about his father's mental health and the father is equally worried about his son. They show this in angry, frustrated rows between them. In addition, the daughter, Susie, has recently returned to live with her father and brother after many years of living with her mother. The mother is not involved in the family therapy sessions so far.

It seems that when I meet with the father and son in the therapy room it is almost impossible to break the cycle of mutual complaint and criticism between them. When I have tried to offer suggestions, these have fallen on deaf ears. Each of them is wedded to their point of view, and neither can step back to be open to alternatives. This describes my view of the family members' responses to each other. But, of course, it is crucial that I also place my thoughts, feelings, and prejudices into the conversational mix.

Not only was I running out of ideas, I did not feel my usual nervous anticipation before meeting with clients. This nervous anticipation is usually a good sign because it means I am prepared for the forthcoming meeting. It makes me alert to what may happen in the session. However, in this instance I was feeling dissatisfied with my attempts to be useful to the clients.

The playback therapy idea came partly as a response to my lack of curiosity. Boredom was creeping in. It was then I ventured to ask my colleagues if they would help me to try something different and, thankfully, they agreed. This was the first step in creating the experimental context for the playback therapy session.

I introduced the playback therapy idea to the family as a way to "do something different as I am feeling a bit at a loss as to how to help take a next step with you." The father and son agreed that we were "not getting anywhere so far."

I set out the schema as follows. First, each therapist would meet with a specified family member in private to hear their views on how the therapy was progressing and to ascertain the clients' views on what themes should be discussed to take the therapy a step forward.

In addition, I asked the therapists paired up with family members to pay attention to their own responses as if entering the character of the client. They would be in a role-play later and asked to enter the client's character as they perceived and experienced it. They were asked not to report as if from the outside about the client, but to be more with the client, as if they were embodying the client rather than simply voicing the client's opinions. They were asked to improvise and avoid any tendency to make a formulation about the client. Instead, they were asked to focus on their feelings, their sensations, and to notice how the client's movements and gestures affected them to try to portray a sense of the client. This has a slightly different emphasis from an ability to try to speak from the "inner voice" of the other. It is intended that this device should be used, but to enrich the voicings through attention to every sense. An intellectualised portrayal is avoided. Instead, the therapist tries to "be" the character. The therapist is encouraged to improvise within the impressions gained in the preliminary individual session with his allocated client.

Following the separate individual sessions with an allocated therapist, the father and son were invited to observe my interview of their respective characters and to comment later on the role-play. In effect, the clients became the team and the team took on the roles of the clients. The family became not only a reflecting team behind a one-way mirror, they were also nominated as critics of our attempt to portray them as best we could.

During the role-play, the therapists entered the improvisation with the freedom to represent their character fully. There was no hidden agenda to educate or point out problematic interactions between father and son. Intentionality was suspended; instead, the client's various perspectives, feelings, wishes, and aims were developed as one might portray characters in a play. My job as interviewer was to conduct the session as I would a family therapy session, and explore without any scripted notion of what direction the conversation should take. I responded in relation to what was offered in the interview, based on the agreed themes of aims, wishes, and expectations of therapy. There was no intention to find solutions, but there was an opportunity to add to the interaction a degree of tolerable risk to contribute words to feelings and impressions that seemed to be on the lips of the clients but somehow were held back between father and son. For example, Paul, the son, wanted the therapy to help his father understand him better and he also wanted someone to help him understand his father better. The therapist role-playing Paul used these exact words and both father and son could hear the conversation that developed in the role-play. Later, Richard, the father, remarked how this observation brought it home to him just how much his son had been trying to help.

After the role-play, both Richard and Paul seemed very moved by the portrayal. It was my hope that the playback role-play might create not just an observer perspective for the clients, but provoke a fresh appraisal of the ways in which the father and son experience their relationship. I wondered if they would notice different perspectives, different emphases in the portrayal from their earlier positions as adversaries. In fact, the role-play seemed to have an emotional impact on the role players, too, and the session was rounded off in an open reflection in which each therapist involved in the role-play was asked to comment on learning that had occurred to them. This question was somewhat unusual, since most therapists feel more at ease when asked to make reflections on the clients they observe. In this playback mode, the therapists enter a role-play that invites their greater immersion in their allocated characters, so to ask about their *own* learning is something of a challenge. One therapist remarked how the portrayal of his character had reminded him of the importance of taking responsibility to do a good job and the role-play had reinforced this belief. Another therapist commented on how important it was to be clear as a father about living daily life as a spiritual person. This theme coincided with the belief of the father in the family, who also wished to lead a more spiritual life. To talk about one's own learning in front of the clients is not to indulge oneself in personal rumination for its own sake. We are present as therapists to assist our clients, so any comment about our own learning must be in the service of useful dialogue for the sake of those seeking our help. It is the promotion of generative ideas and shared experiences that contribute to potential developments. In this instance, the father and son helped me and the team to assist them further by moving beyond the therapeutic impasses I identified at the beginning of the session.

Some pointers to heed if trying out playback therapy

The pairing up session (in this case for about fifteen minutes) allows for a closer appreciation of the individual family member's position, and creates a working alliance with the paired up therapist to portray the family member's views sensitively and respectfully. Family members not only indicate what matters to them about their aims and expectations of therapy, but, in so doing, they are actively giving the therapist a commission to represent their views in the coming role-play.

Being invited behind the one-way mirror to sit where the therapist team usually sits is also an act that literally changes perspective, and potentially alters perceived power relations between team and family through a more transparent and intimate arrangement of co-operative practice.

Without the client's ability to take a risk with us, the experiment would fail. In this case, both father and son took their positions as "team members" very seriously, so the atmosphere between all participants felt collaborative and jointly experimental.

In addition to what is discussed between client and therapist, the therapist can begin to sense possible themes that are "not yet said" but are somehow implicit in the one-to-one discussions. These are the nuances that point, perhaps, to a more creative and novel dialogue between participants that might emerge in the role-play to follow. The therapist attempts to enter the logic of the family member's views and also tries to embody their experience. This provides the material to be portrayed in the forthcoming playback role-play. For instance, the therapist who attended to the son's wish to be better understood by his father and for his father to be better understood by the son was developed in the subsequent role-play. It stood out as a relevant relational theme to portray and explore.

The direction of the role-play cannot be overly structured. The role players offered their portrayals as family members in response to my questions about their experience of the therapy so far, and their expectations about the next possible steps. Most of all, the role-play avoids any crass instructive interaction that could be construed by the family members as a strategic educational illustration on how to get along better. The emphasis is on portraying from within the familiar experiences of the family as they are portrayed.

Family members observing themselves portrayed sensitively allows for private reflection on the observed role play and possibilities for fresh dialogue (in this case, between father and son). By inviting the clients to observe and later participate via their critique, we attempt to make the disparity between client and therapist somewhat less of a power differential. Following the role-play, when we all gathered together to comment on our own learning, Richard said, "I don't feel so alone. I can understand Paul better as you portrayed my family . . . not only as it is but how I want it to be . . ."

In this mode, the one-way mirror acts as a proscenium arch rather than an evaluative, objectivising frame. We are playing a little with the idea of expertise. When family members are invited to become critics of the therapists' role-play from behind the one-way mirror, we take a further step towards irreverence. Implicit is the notion of co-creativity as a context; not creativity as if it resides in the heads of experts. Our expertise is in trying to find creative possibilities within the contexts of our practice. In playback therapy, the usual hierarchy is playfully reversed. The family becomes the team. The team becomes a characterisation of the family, and the family members are always afforded the last word.

Summary of main stages in playback therapy

Stage one:	discussion with family members.
Stage two:	pairing up sessions (one therapist and one family member).
Stage three:	role-play with family as observing team.
Stage four:	family invited to offer responses: critique of role-play.
Stage five (optional):	all role players and family members to offer final reflections (therapists invited here to comment on their own learning).

This mode of practice actively encourages the role-playing therapists to pay greater attention to their embodied responsiveness as they meet with the clients. The significance of embodied responsiveness as a rich resource for the performance of systemic practice and supervision is creatively explored in Bownas and Fredman (2017) and is here illustrated to offer you some modes to play with.

Performative modes of supervision

Useful and creative sources of possibility in supervision can occur where the focus includes the effect of practice on emotional, embodied responses and ethical dilemmas of the supervisee and supervisor. Processes of supervision require us to move beyond simple instructive interaction, with its assumptions about power and expertise being seen to reside within the expert supervisor; Freire's criticism of "banking education" is a parallel already discussed. The dimensions of race, culture, gender and class that are latent and/or active in the supervisory relationship is fully explored in Burck and Daniel (2010) in recognising how supervisor and supervisee may be "positioned" in relation to one another and, in turn, positioned within the organisational context of practice. Supervision within a systemic humanist orientation sits comfortably with a focus and critique on how power relations are construed and enacted in any encounter in life. This is very different from forms of supervision that avoid an analysis of power relations and describe clients as one might describe a painting hanging on a wall; instead, the practitioner is *in* the picture of practice, so to speak, not set aside from it. This does not imply that management supervision or other forms of professional regulation are forgotten or unnecessary—quite the contrary; clients' rights, and professional standards must be upheld and concerned with ethical practice.

The following are illustrations of modes in which performative supervision is introduced and where constraints on creativity are made evident and explored.

The harassed practitioner

A colleague comes for supervision; he has many files and notes to describe the cases he wishes to talk about. I can see that he is anxious as he fumbles to find the notes of the session he wishes to discuss first. I listen to the urgency in his voice as he explains how he carried out the appropriate measures and check-lists about his young client's depression and anxiety levels. There seemed little space to pause and ask any questions about what he wanted from me in this case.

The formulations came thick and fast; the agreement to set goals for each session clearly set out. However, there was no sense of a connection between the therapist and the client, and very little sense of my connection with the supervisee. I could not gauge whether this practice had engaged the family members. Certainly, they had complied with all the required documentation, but they were somehow absent from our session. There was no sense of the therapist's presence other than as a note taker and form filler. Now, I know my colleague is a caring practitioner, but the quality of the discussion was confined to what John Shotter refers to as "about-ness talk", as if we existed separately from our participation in our observations. More importantly, the quality of "manualised" talk devalued the attempt by my colleague to help the family concerned. He and I were at risk of limiting the conversation to rational descriptions of the client's situation. I felt I was being invited to become a technician to help with his technical difficulties in finding an appropriate next technical step to take. Everything had become "technologised", including my responses to my colleague. So, I asked, "What are your hopes for your work with this child?"

The supervisee began to place his hopes for therapy within a more relational frame, including his difficulties in creating a safe enough working alliance with the child and his family. The focus shifted from a consideration of specific techniques to one in which the intricacies of his attempts to form a working alliance allowed him to refocus on his part in the interactional process. This changed the focus from objective descriptors of the child's problems towards more relationally focused themes. It also created a more professionally intimate and co-operative connection between us. Hope emerged as a focus. We began to feel something could develop just as we began to make the supervision more alive, more *vital*, to explore possibilities between us.

Enquiries that invite exploration of the supervisee's imagination can engender greater compassion and sympathy for the clients by trying to think about the *life* of the client—their vitality, wishes, and hopefulness, as well as the wider context of their lives. By changing the angle of enquiry, we began to evoke a different conversation and, hence, a different view of the client in the context of her relationship with the therapist.

Contextual tensions in supervision

This example also draws attention to the wider context of the supervisory relationship, since I was also part of the organisation that was funding practitioners to be trained in a model that focused on the individual almost exclusively. Both the supervisee and I had to contend with this organisational challenge. To bring this challenge into our discussion was necessary, since the scope and constraints of supervision were affected by organisational demands for additional training. In effect, I was being asked to do something outside my remit. The agency had been pushing for training courses sponsored by IAPT, and, however useful they might turn out to be, the effect was to substantially deplete the workforce, resulting in the remaining staff being expected to fill the gaps in service and supervision. This attempt to meet demands for supervision with increasingly limited resources found expression in the micro-relational features of the interaction with my colleague. Drawing attention to isomorphic processes within the supervisory relationship, and between the agency and the staff group, helped us to address the wider contextual features playing out between us in supervision. (See, for example, Partridge, 2010.) In discussion with the supervisee, I could consider what was possible within supervision that would satisfy the demands of the organisation, yet not unduly compromise the systemic nature of supervision I could provide. Clarification of the scope and purpose of family therapy supervision included elaboration of the misfit between expectations of systemic supervision and a model of practice that I had no experience to supervise. In this case, I clarified with the manager of the team that training in individually focused models of practice would be provided by a trained professional in that model.

Ideally, supervision and practice are sources of stimulation to be enjoyed, not endured. When we are absorbed in a creative exploration, we feel lifted. We have more resources at our fingertips. We have an idea or two to help us to take the next step with the client. On the other hand, the heavily manualised supervisee will feel constrained to talk of his attempts to loyally implement the objectives and practices of a manual. This should not stop supervisors from both respecting what manualised treatments may offer in direction and general applicability, but neither should they confine opportunities to look at the unique circumstances of each client and family.

This places a responsibility on the supervisor to give permission to the supervisee to be a freer thinker. The context shifts from one of checks and balances towards intersubjective matters. This shift is not a wild diversion from serious matters; it is, in fact, a way of homing in on what is possible in the actuality of practice and supervision. Theories about causes and treatments are considered with respect but held as potentially useful ideas, not truths, to explore possibilities for fresh perspectives that enliven our practice.

The harassed practitioner knew of other perspectives, but the power of managerialism and surveillance organised the way in which we first talked about the clients. The growing tendency towards placing protocols and policies before client need threatens practice as a process of humanisation.

Aesthetic practices are context specific

Imagination invigorates serious conversation. To invite the play of ideas, with metaphor and story, fanciful associations and humour, loosens the ties of overly formulaic practice. To let go of standardised practices and protocols can be risky and one needs to feel secure enough as a practitioner to begin to improvise as if on the spur of the moment. The systemic humanist practitioner does not avoid protocols and models when they contribute usefully to creative direction in practice. The question is to consider when and under what circumstances standardised procedures are useful for the clients' benefit and when they simply fail to deal with the level of responsiveness their difficulties demand. Risk averse and objectifying practices in supervision are components that distance the practitioner from creative thinking and action. On the other hand, performative modes employed within supervision offer another route to promote fresh experiences and freer thinking about possibilities.

Personifying important themes

My heart tells me one thing, my head another!

This is an example from supervision that enabled a trainee practitioner to explore his mixed feelings about a family he was meeting. The practitioner described feeling torn between continuing to support a child at home with his parents yet also feeling totally responsible for the child's welfare. Should he report his concerns to the social services, which might break the family's trust in him, or should he continue to be a supportive link for the child and hope that matters would improve in time?

We discussed his worries about what to do. He said at one point, "My heart tells me to keep involved supporting the child but my head says I must inform the social services of my worries."

I asked him to pick two colleagues from the group, one to become the character of "Your Head" and one to become the character of "Your Heart". This he did.

I then asked if there were other important themes to register. He chose another group member to represent his "Hope" and another to speak from the position of the "Overseeing Authority".

I asked him then to place the four characters around him, seated as in a group interview, with each character placed in proximity to the supervisee to represent their importance to him, like the technique of family sculpting (see Walrond-Skinner, 1976)). He took time to arrange the characters around him, and when he was satisfied with the seating arrangements I talked with him while the characters listened in. I explored his thoughts on the impact of each character on his practice. The style of exploration is like that described in the playback therapy example above. Some sample questions were:

- When you listen to your Head, what does it advise?
- When Heart and Head are in discussion, what sort of things do they debate/disagree about?
- When you talk about Overseeing Authority, are there times when it feels good to have him/her present?
- Does Hope always "spring eternal", or does it leave you alone at times? And if so, when does this happen?

I followed this exploration of the relative influences of each character on the supervisee by inviting each character's responses and reflections on what they had heard him say, before returning to the supervisee.

As he listened to the conversation between the four characters and me, he began to get a much clearer idea about the relational processes between each theme. Overseeing Authority, Hope, Head, and Heart, were all in "conversation", rather than considered, fixed states in opposition to one another.

In this instance, the trainee came to the decision to talk with the parents about his concerns for their child's welfare, alongside his wish to continue to support them. He decided he should not shoulder responsibility for statutory services, and would discuss these with a social work colleague.

The portrayal of the four characters in the presence of the supervisee enabled him to come to a fresh appraisal of his practice quandary in much the same way as the father and son came to a fresh appreciation of one another in the playback session; the supervisee allowed himself to stand back and experience his quandary from a different position. An alternative response could simply have been to advise him to bring his dilemma to the relevant authority, and he might have complied with this advice. However, I did not consider the advice would have respected the depth of feeling his dilemma had upon him. Perhaps he would have complied, but my guess is he would have done so without an internal conviction that would carry his work forward. In coming to the decision via the performative mode of exploratory supervision, he owned the decision for himself.

Consultation as performative, relational exploration

To set a contrast: typically, in case presentations in busy mental health teams, a client's situation is presented and opinions sought from the multi-disciplinary group that is present. In my experience, the most senior group members' views are given most attention, and debates usually occur around the supposed causes and focus of intervention. This a form of consultation that can be useful when the presenter wants clear direction about where to access a route to further services, or is seeking a straightforward clarification of a particular matter. However, when the consultation is more to do with gaining ideas and suggestions about how to take the next step in therapy, the matter becomes more complex. Attempts to provide clear direction or instruction to the consultee can result in a conflict of opinion because the intricacy of the client's context, and the practitioner's part in the overall relational system, is not given sufficient attention. In this situation, it becomes problematic when trying to impose "about-ness" talk where "with-ness" talk is more useful. This is not to suggest that one is necessarily better than the other, simply that each form of dialogue places emphasis on different aspects of practice. When talk *about* clients fails to attend to the complexity of the relational context within which the biases and orientation of the practitioner are overlooked, the consultation misses the key question, "How might this consultation be useful to *you* in your thinking and experience of working with your clients/patients?"; that is, refusing to objectify the clients by separating them off from the biases/prejudices/formulations of the professional seeking consultation.

For ideas to be useful in practice, they must have some application that can be followed through. If a consultee feels her endeavours are not receiving sufficient respect, the chances are that consultation can become deskilling for the presenter fearful of being exposed for not doing a good enough job. At worst, practitioners can feel scrutinised, or even persecuted by responses which only offer opinions and ideas that are disconnected from the unique quality of the working alliance with the client. The consultation has missed the connection between the human being of the practitioner and her client, and instead has opted for discussion of "disembodied" ideas about what to do. When ideas compete with one another without taking account of the complexity of praxis, they remain abstract and do not translate into utility.

In contrast, the following example introduces elements of play, the active engagement of group members' imagination, and a systemic exploration through a performative mode for case consultation. The remit was clear: I had been asked to facilitate the multi-disciplinary case presentations, so I have been given permission, negotiated with my colleagues in the management group, to provide this service to the team. I appreciate that not all colleagues have the same freedom to explore performative systemic modes of consultation but, nevertheless, a degree of experimentalism in consultation is possible if negotiated in time with supportive colleagues.

In this instance, my colleague wishes to discuss a case where she is concerned about which direction to take.

I begin by interviewing her about her wishes for the aim of the group consultation, "So we can focus precisely on what you consider to be the most important theme/s for us to attend to."

After describing briefly the context of practice and the client family's predicaments, she states that there are four themes on which she would like our views because they have an impact on her uncertainty about which direction to take next.

She identifies these as: a perspective on *hope* for change, a *medical opinion*, a view on how *gender* relationships shape the work, and a perspective on how *race* or racism is affecting the child at the centre of the case.

I ask if it would be all right to try something a little different from her usual ways of exploring a case presentation. I ask her, "Could you please select four group members to 'speak' from the character of Gender, Race, Hope, and Medicine?"

The atmosphere lightens; there is some laughter and a playfulness that suggests it is safe enough to try this. Each member is selected by the presenter to represent the given theme, and there is general levity when the medical consultant is selected to be the character of "Medicine". She objects and says, "I want to be someone else for a change!" To do justice to the selection, I also asked the presenter to place each character around her to represent their closeness or influence upon her thinking. This uses ideas from family sculpting combined with elements of externalisation (White & Epston, 1990).

The joke from my colleague from psychiatry relaxed the atmosphere. In effect, we were beginning to play. It was a breakthrough moment; people were more relaxed, and openly expressive to seriously play. Participants eased into their roles, personifying the themes outlined by the presenter.

As a first step, the consultant interviews the consultee using exploratory, contextualising questions about each of the themes and their impact on the presenter's thinking about the case. For example:

- In what way is the voice of [the character, Medicine, Hope, etc.] useful to you in this case?
- How does [the character] impact on your practice in constraining ways? How do you explain this to yourself?
- If [the character] were to be in a more useful relationship to you, how would this come about?
- In comparing the four characters, how do you think they talk to each other?
- How much influence does [the character] have on your views of how to help the family?

Once these and other contextualising questions are posed, the consultee is invited to offer her reflections, should she wish to add some comment at this point.

In the meantime, the four characters have been sitting listening, and the second step is to begin to create a relationally focused interview of the four characters to hear their feelings, views, and general responses as they each listened to the co-interview about their part in the context. At this point, the presenter is asked to "sit back and listen to the responses from the four characters as I talk with them."

The third step, of interviewing each of the four characters, is not easy to prescribe, but the consultant's role here is to elicit each response, and to invite comparison, agreement, questions, hypothetical questions, questions that aim to generate fresh ideas, all the time keeping an eye on the presenter to see if she is becoming curious about what and how the characters are "performing". Examples are:

Consultant (to Hope): When you hear Gender describe how difficult it is to bring her voice into the sessions, how to you respond?

Hope: I think Gender could take a few more risks because [the presenter] has the trust of the family, and she can now push a little more on that score.

Consultant (to Medicine): When you hear Hope talk about taking more risks, where does that place your concerns?

Medicine: I am cautious because I am needed for the time being to support the mother and stabilise her depression.

This portrayal need only take five or ten minutes, with the aim of developing useful ideas based on the exploration of the themes and their interconnections affecting the consultee's practice.

Finally, the consultant invites responses from the consultee while the characters sit in silence. Usually, this form of joint exploration also benefits from asking each character to debrief by saying a few words about any learning points they might have taken from the exercise for their own practice.

In this example, I recall that many useful ideas were expressed and considered in relation to what was practically possible from the consultee's point of view. The voice of Hope struck a chord with the practitioner, who generated her own next steps in the work with the family.

In this performative form of consultation, the reductionist language of diagnosis was utilised, and placed, within a relational context. Medicine was important and was present in relation to other characters portrayed. Furthermore, the portrayal had an audience of the multi-disciplinary team, who observed and had opinions to offer in the final discussion. This proved to be a useful extension to other forms of consultation within the team, and one that was usually entered into with a sense of collegiate co-operation and enjoyment.

This form of consultation, if not over used, encourages freedom of expression without the need to be correct. The intolerance of uncertainty that can come when practitioners are desperately seeking answers was replaced by the entertainment of uncertainty: to consider that all views could be useful as part of a developing, co-creative context so long as it results in us doing a better job.

The capacity to have serious matters addressed with a light touch is not to diminish the seriousness. The point is that the humour, the stimulation of the imagination, are constituents of conversation that not only humanise and respect the patient's situation, but also allow for more openly humanising, joint experiences between team members.

Most of the examples outlined involved multi-actor participation, but, on many occasions, the style of improvisational, performative, and experimental aspects in supervision can be adapted to one-to-one supervision and practice where the supervisor–practitioner roles change position, as in reversals and role-plays, becoming characters representing a dominant or problematic theme, inviting the client/supervisee to indulge this characterisation temporarily to see what emerges. To play with ideas is to wake up to aesthetic practice, and to wake up *from* the stultifying effects of anaesthetic practice.

The client becomes a benign character to help her mother

In one closing session of family therapy, after the young person's anxiety problems had sufficiently abated, the mother in the family spoke up.

"Now as we are ending, I begin to think I pressured Jenny (the sixteen-year-old client) too much. I am a perfectionist and my Protestant work ethic gets the better of me."

I took this an as invitation to shift the focus, and asked the mother if she would like to explore the positives, as well as the limitations, of her Protestant work ethic. I also sympathised with her—"I know what you mean!"

She agreed. I invited Jenny to be the character of "your mother's Protestant work ethic."

The young person was slightly surprised, but liked the idea of not being the "patient". I described what I wanted her to try to do along the lines of the creativity exercise outlined in Chapter Three except, on this occasion, the client is helping her mother to consider her mother's self-defined "Protestant work ethic", which she said was creating a barrier to her daughter by being too hard on her.

We are playing. The choice of the character of "Protestant Work Ethic" (PWE) allows for a more exploratory discussion on the benefits and limitations rather than being restricted to the negative connotation the mother offers of being too much of a perfectionist who pressures her daughter too much. There is more room to avoid unnecessary criticism of the mother as a person; rather, the PWE is a part of her cultural and religious experience that she brought into the conversation. The character of PWE was already identified by her as part of her repertoire in responding to her daughter. The exercise created some laughter from both mother and daughter and led to open discussion about how PWE interrupted the positive sides of their relationship so that PWE would be less domineering in the future.

These novel ways of creating a fresh stage in therapy is not to decry other active ways of utilising drama or "action methods". However, what I want to emphasise here is the attention to relational processes between all participants that lies at the heart of a systemic humanising orientation. Some illustrations have similarities with other methods from different theoretical approaches. The congruent features are not contentious but the expressions of experimental improvisational and performative practices here described are built on systemic foundations.

Be wary of the magician

Samuels (2015) makes a bid for a therapist not to be too self-critical. Failure is a necessary and inevitable part of the process of healing. A self-critical analysis is a prompt towards failing better. Samuels calls for therapists to be given room to roam in psychotherapy. The irreverent therapist can be part of us all, but is sometimes cowed by authority, deference, and fear of showing itself. Samuels refers to the irreverent practitioner as the Trickster, a term I do not feel comfortable with since a "Trickster" can trick himself into thinking this is the best way to act as a practitioner, and that would be a mistake. Hubris is a killer of co-creativity. The hubristic, clever therapist is more likely to be impressed with his cleverness than paying attention to the client's responses.

The hubristic therapist stands in contrast to the view that psychology and psychotherapy can make useful, yet modest, claims to success (Smail, 2006). Keeney (2009) implores therapists to avoid the social sciences altogether, and be concerned instead with therapeutic healing as an ancient and performative art. He invites therapists to

> take pride in being an artist. You are part of a great historical tradition of aesthetic performance, with roots that go way further than Vienna. Before psychology, psychiatry, and social work, there were performers whose creative expression healed others. (p. 265)

It is an intriguing invitation, and somewhat seductive. But, for me, this emphasis distracts attention from the social structures that create, maintain, or contribute significantly to human distress, as well as placing overemphasis on the therapist's contribution to healing. It is a therapist-centred claim to hold exclusive expertise and/or "magical" qualities. This places the locus of healing between the therapist and client, underemphasising the context within which people who care about each other can make important changes that include the services of a therapist on occasion. It is the context that counts, not the individual creativity or performative ability, solely, of the practitioner. Keeney's concept of the "creative therapist" separates the so-called run-of-the-mill practitioner (that is, all of us) from the priesthood of therapeutic magicians. Instead, I prefer to see the improvisational, experimentalist practitioner as embedded in systemic humanising principles that promote co-creativity between all participants. Creativity, here, holds a broader definition as creativity-in-context.

Demonstrating what not to do . . . by default

To guard against hubris, and to remind myself of the merits of systemic humility, here is an illustration of features that can ensure that an attempt at contrived spontaneity is a mistake.

Haarlem, Holland. The workshop is full of experienced practitioners; I have been holding a two-day workshop on improvisation and the development of performative practices in family therapy. On the afternoon of the second day, I have agreed to provide a live demonstration to the audience, who sit in the same large lecture room as me.

The family arrives; they look very annoyed with their accompanying therapist, and with each other. Anneka, the young person at the centre of concerns, is a particularly angry-looking sixteen-year-old girl. I try to make everyone welcome but I am already anxious that this is going to be a tricky session, and I also feel I must "pull a rabbit out of the hat" to demonstrate what I have been teaching for a day and a half.

The session does not go well. The beginning is rushed, and I do not feel I have had time to acquaint myself with the reasons that this family has been invited. The more I try to encourage participation, the less participative the family members become.

I decide I will invite Anneka (who is looking increasingly disgruntled) to sit behind me, and that I would then attempt to ask questions that I imagined might be on her mind, to put to her divorcing parents. To my relief, she does as I ask; I think perhaps now we will get somewhere.

I began to "demonstrate" one of the modes I have outlined in the workshop—that of the client as consultant to the therapist. I suggested that the young person should interrupt me at any time should she wish to put a question to me which I would place before her increasingly awkward-looking parents. It was as if I could not stop from carrying on with this performance despite my feeling that it was not getting anywhere. Then, to my great relief, the girl tapped me on the shoulder; I turned to her expectantly, thinking, "this could be a good move", only to see her glowering face as she said, "Why are you asking all these *stupid* questions?" Here was my comeuppance for my hubris.

It was, indeed, a very good question and one that helped me to reposition my endeavours and complete the session, saving face by first acknowledging her question and offering some explanation. I said something like, "Good question, Anneka . . . I'm asking these questions in the hope of trying to be useful to you and your family because everybody looks so down." This, at least, allowed us to address the "music" in the family's presentation, and from there we began to make a slightly better connection.

The learning stays with me. Each time we try, our endeavours should be couched in doing what is possible, rather than feeling bound by hubris or defined protocol to implement a plan that no one else is following. It was a classic mistake to try to fit technique awkwardly into a context instead of waiting to see what might be more useful to do. When we fail, the aim should be to fail better next time.

The magician therapist is an a-political creation; there is no analysis of the political, cultural, and societal interests at work on the production of human distress. In our post welfare state, we are being pedalled a myth that individual endeavour is all that is required to insure against distress or need; that psychological "distress" is addressed by individual cure and carried out by an expert who holds the skill to impart the curative method. This mentality sets people against one another; we extract them from their social context and place them, largely, inside a hermetically sealed bubble, the internalisation of all that is problematic. The danger of the magician therapist or practitioner is seeing creativity also as a hermetically sealed, internal quality.

Time to pause

It is not easy when we are seen to hold expertise, to admit to failings and downright errors, especially if we feel our work is under scrutiny, where errors are thought of as weaknesses or signs of incompetence. But this is important to face up to because practice is more of a craft than a science. We meet our clients as human beings, not as an experiment made *upon* them but to improvise and experiment *with* them, in joint action. Even when manuals are available or prescribed to us as a way of working, we can find them useful if we also have freedom to improvise within the unique qualities of our meetings with each client. We cannot fail to improvise because each moment we are, in effect, creating something new in our dealings with one another. The question, in times of financial and organisational constraints, is to investigate the degree to which our freedom to experiment is confined.

There is a cartoon of a fly buzzing around in a bottle and eventually the fly sees that the neck of the bottle is open and thinks, "At last! Freedom from this confined space!" As he buzzes his way out of the bottle, the cartoon pans back only to reveal that our free fly has simply entered a slightly bigger bottle. The question posed at the beginning of the book, "Do I recognise myself in the job I do?" is pertinent here. When we critically appraise the possibilities and limitations placed on our practice, we also glimpse that there is something better on the horizon, even if that horizon is itself circumscribed.

Power relations set limits on possibility

No discussion of practice or supervision is adequate without attention to how power is expressed and enacted in organisations and between us in our social relations. The central importance of one's position and commission within the organisation is crucial in shaping possibilities and constraints on our practice. In Salamon and McCarthy's work with child protection services, they draw attention to the need to clarify the contradictory expectations of the practitioner who is simultaneously given a commission to support families and to investigate possible, or actual, child abuse. By clarifying the practitioner's remit, and distinguishing between these twin tasks, ". . . we feel that we can become more transparent in relation to our systemic positioning and involvements" (Salamon & McCarthy, 2016, p. 287). Our commission, as practitioners, is always in need of clarification. Who is the client? How much co-operation is possible for mutually shared goals, and how much is agreed between professionals where clients simply comply or are opposition?

> We, as supervisors, therapists and social workers are inevitably part of the frame of analysis. A commission is therefore clarified per the situation and place in which one is living and working, and is never based on objective criteria. (Salamon & McCarthy, 2016, p. 287)

In all the examples illustrated here, the first and most important stage was to work towards making both practice and supervision a safe enough setting in which to improvise. The features of building this safety in teamwork require the practitioner to become a "possibilist", and for that sense of possibilism to be fuelled by a systemic humanising orientation to practice, especially so in situations where organisational and job remits limit co-operative practices. We enact systemic principles; they do not simply reside as abstract ideas. Without seeing practice as a process of mutual humanisation calling on joint action and connection between us, the likelihood of creating a safe enough context is limited. It takes time and effort.

In the next chapter, I consider the strength of forces that would and do conspire to thwart co-creativity. They are identified to promote debate and critical action, to enrich and inspire a more systemically humanising orientation to mental health and social care. What we stand for also tells us about what we stand against.

CHAPTER SIX

Forces that push us from behind

The morning begins with coffee and a chat with some of my colleagues, who are already seated at their computers by 8.15 a.m. A new habit of entering the exact time of arrival and departure has emerged in recent weeks, and a new form of "presentism" has appeared. There is a joke about who gets the prize for being first at their desk each morning. Behind the humour is a feeling of being scrutinised. To "wake up and smell the coffee" has never had such relevance. The temptation is to go straight into the email correspondence, and attend to a never-ending stream of requirements in the "must dos" of administration.

This sets the scene for an increasing number of dedicated practitioners in social care and mental health. The forces that push us from behind is a metaphor for the pressures created by distal processes that have an influence on how we think and function in our jobs and, more generally, in our lives. Fromm sees our awareness of such forces as the first step in altering our circumstances. It is a belief

> in the possibility that a course already initiated can be altered. This possibility of change [is] rooted in man's capacity for becoming aware of the forces which move him behind his back so to speak—and thus enabling him to regain his freedom. (Fromm, 1964, p. 124)

These forces have been addressed in each of the foregoing chapters, as they are experienced in the proximity of daily practice. Here, I emphasise a view on how distal forces operate to influence the broader contexts of practice within which we work. So long as these forces remain invisible or absent from our discussion, we are more likely to be unaware of just how strong the pushes from the back can become. The historical–political precedents to the current state of affairs in mental health provision and their impact on the culture within the NHS and mental health services are addressed.

Constraints on creativity are not only financial, but are the result of shifts in the cultural values and dominant discourses which have arrived with the commodification of care, and the crude application of business principles to human caring professions. These include the persistence of a discourse that places emphasis on individual pathology and diagnostic categorisation as the main locus of a person's expression of distress. To avoid the wider cultural and structural influences on a person's difficulties is a glaring omission, as is a failure to recognise and act to change the impact of structural reorganisation on service delivery. The systemic nature of cuts and constraints directly affects the functioning of practitioners and the clients who use the services. To do what is required ethically to uphold professional practice demands that we ask questions of ourselves and of others as to whether we will creatively disobey in order to maintain humanising practices.

By naming the forces pushing us from the back, we can begin to consider how to relate more actively to the impact they have upon us; in short, we choose to push back, resist, offer alternatives, or step aside.

A push from behind: bureaucratisation breaks human connections

At one community mental health hospital in which I worked, a fire alarm went off during a busy day. We all trooped out into the car park, slightly pleased to have a break in the fresh air. When the head count was made at the assembly point, there were seventy hospital staff and only two patients. This illustration receives many nods of confirmation from colleagues from a cross-section of social care and mental health services who are worried about the decrease in opportunities to be directly involved in face-to-face contact with clients. The effect is quite literally to distance clients from those employed to help them. Waiting lists for mental health services are long, and demand is high. Clients often wait months to see a mental health practitioner. To counter this problem, procedures are put in place to cut waiting lists to try to meet clients more promptly and carefully. However, in trying to solve this problem, others are created as the task becomes focused on statistics to reduce waiting list times, juggling figures rather than meeting with people in ways that are useful to them. In practice, such attempts to streamline services disrupt continuity and increase bureaucratic demands that limit face-to-face contact. Completing the appropriate forms and computerised records can take precedence over establishing a sound therapeutic alliance with new clients. Clearly, this is not what practitioners or their managers wish to do, and neither is it helpful to new clients meeting this form of disjointed service delivery. But, statistically, such procedures look impressive; more clients are seen more quickly and the necessary aims and "pathways" are set out and measurable, except this is mostly smoke and mirrors. Clients might be seen more quickly in the first instance but they often languish on an internal waiting list until their case can be allocated. This raises expectations that help will be provided only to have the door tantalisingly closed after one or two initial assessment sessions.

The rationale that such statistics can help to establish the demand for a service is understandable; having a measure of demand is a necessary tool in helping policy makers and practitioners to assess need and service priorities. However, the tools to measure create categories of diagnosis that serve as a ticket to access services largely geared towards a bio-medical analysis of a person's difficulties.

Counting statistics of problem definition might assist in helping to identify gaps in service delivery but, if the definition of a problem is located largely within the individual patient, the statistics fail to fully consider the social and relational contributions to human distress. Team meetings that purport to allow time for case discussion can become overtaken by talk of the latest procedure that one must complete, or discussion of the labyrinthine sub-categories of individual diagnosis. In addition, practitioners are placed in a somewhat contradictory position when required to complete measurements of outcome. Many of the measurement forms serve two incompatible purposes: the first is to support client feedback and therapeutic alliance, and the second to support an organisation's psychometric data collection, which managers and commissioners use to assess the efficacy of a service. There is a paradox here: in the middle is the practitioner who is asked to use the forms to invite honest, useful, client feedback that can help us fine-tune our work together, and our service, including comments about what we might do better together. On the other hand, the practitioner is also asked use these forms to show how "well" the team or service is doing, thus inviting positive, encouraging feedback.

Attempts have been made by researchers in recent years to challenge such reductive and individualised measures (Rober, 2015; Seikkula & Arnkil, 2014; Simon & Chard, 2014: Stratton, 2016; Sundet, 2012, 2014; Wampold, 2011). However, predominant research methods mainly focus on definable outcomes for specific, individually focused, behaviourally measurable problems; they lack consideration of wider relationally and contextually focused *processes* of change.

By way of an example illustrative of the limitations of reducing our vision to individual categories of diagnosis, consider the following case.

The three-generational bugbear

I meet with a boy called Tim who is frightened to go to school because he is worried that bugs will make him sick. He has already missed many days in primary school, and will soon be faced with the transition to a large comprehensive school. He is small and slim and he tells me that the "bugs are invisible". His mother anxiously watches me talking with her son.

I enquire if he could invent a spray that would get rid of bugs, "... just enough so you can go out more".

He looks interested in the idea and devises an invisible spray that will kill off bugs.

He explains that the spray is "self-refilling" when I ask him if it will run out of bug-killing juice. The mother looks at me as if I am a little crazy to talk like this with her son but, at the next session, the bug spray seems to have had a therapeutic effect, and the boy manages to attend the start of comprehensive school the following month.

Everything seems well and, given the long waiting list, the case could now be closed.

Everything *is* well, except that this is where the positive measure of success reveals its limitations. While at comprehensive school, Tim begins to struggle to cope with the demands of large classes. He falls behind, and is eventually suspended. His confidence is at a low ebb. His parents are anxious and angry at the lack of alternative provision for him. We continue to meet, though his father does not participate in the sessions. In time, I negotiate a place in a small school, designed to offer a sensitive service to children who are fearful of groups and open places.

Let us pause here. How might one begin to analyse the complexity of the individual, family, and social features of this boy's problems? Certainly, I could have closed the case when he made the transition to comprehensive school. I would have satisfied the requisite measures and outcomes. It was a success. But, of course, his life was much more complicated than such crude measures could convey.

Now let us move on some months. Tim is gaining confidence in his new school; the teachers are dealing with him in a welcoming, sensitive, but challenging way. He is thriving. But at home he is withdrawn and does not socialise much. I make home visits and learn from the father that he lost his job several years ago, and is, himself, frightened to be out in the world. He panics and cannot get beyond the garden gate without a great deal of support from his wife. I ask about what help he has received. "I was given a programme to follow but I couldn't follow it because I couldn't do it on my own."

The more I understood about Tim's life as a young, nervous boy, the more I appreciated his courage and, latterly, the courage of his father, in taking small steps to break away from the confines of their lives. At the last session, the father commented that his own mother "had not been out of the house for fifteen years before she died".

Tim's distress, expressed in fearfulness, is one illustration amongst countless others who deserve their problems to be responded to by a systemic humanising approach. To simply diagnose Tim as school phobic, or consider his father depressed, would be to restrict an analysis to individualised, diagnostic categories. Yet, these are sometimes descriptors used by practitioners whose practice has become reactive rather than reflective, distancing from the emotional experience and complex interactions of the clients. What ultimately assisted Tim and his family was the provision of a family-based service and the support of a small educational establishment geared to help children like Tim. The social relational context was of much greater significance in his development than any short-term, individualised "intervention" to help him deal with his fears.

In another illustration from my work in a mental health service, I received three separate referrals on three children from the same family. In addition, both the father and mother were involved with the adult mental health services. I was instructed that each person required their own file with individual treatment plans set out and records kept in each file after every session. Had I fully complied with these "must dos" to the letter, I would have spent one hour seeing the family and at least two hours inserting all the notes, and completing all the checks and balances for statistical purposes. Fortunately, my manager helped me to find a way to streamline some of this bureaucratic spaghetti and still satisfy the administrative demand. But the problem here is that by spending so much time on the paperwork, I was seen to be doing the right thing. In fact, I could well have used more time to meet with the family, who were in dire need of co-ordinated, attentive, and regular support.

Another push: the impact of privatisation and commodification

Aneurin Bevan, the key politician who pursued the implementation of the National Health Service, commented on the danger of putting a price on a person's health when he wrote,

> Danger of abuse in the health service is not in the way that ordinary people use the service. Abuse is always at the point where private commercialism impinges on the services . . . where an attempt is made to marry the incompatible principles of private profit with public service. The solution is to decrease the dependence on private enterprise . . . A free health service is a triumphant example of the superiority of the principles of collective action and public initiative against the commercial principle of profit and greed. (1952, p. 88)

Sixty years later, the political philosopher Michael Sandel makes the same argument in criticising the money markets for their impact on human relationships. When care comes with a price tag, the impact on those caught up in the marketisation of care can "dull [their] ethical sensibilities" (2012, p. 141).

Models, manuals, and measurements

Part of the growing glare of financial scrutiny of effectiveness and evidence-based practice is the spotlight on therapy models, and the use of manuals that purport to be cost effective and efficient. Effectiveness, measurable outcomes, and efficiency are all laudable aims, but they can also tip towards an over focus on formulaic interventions that contradict clinical judgement and ethical practice. Practitioners might be asked to cut corners, and work with short-term interventions that they believe will only gloss over more profound distress.

Models of practice, protocols, and techniques are often manualised, and they can have a useful place in service delivery to ground practice with ideas of useful directions to take. They can help practitioners to develop technical skills in carrying out particular aspects of the manualised approach, but what they do not do is teach relational competences, and they have the tendency to turn practitioners into technicians following plans set out by manualised steps and stages. Yet, how we interact at any given moment in response to the other is a relational ability that is crucial and not able to be prescribed; rather, it asks what the context invites from us, and this is a much more subtle and nuanced process.

There is an important distinction to be made between manuals that insist on strict "fidelity" and those that offer more flexibility. A manual is to practice as a musical score is to playing music. A musician brings the music to life by playing while paying attention to other musicians, the audience, and the nuances of her interpretation, feelings, and spontaneous responses when improvisation occurs. If played as a formula, the results are mechanistic, and bereft of connection with the audience. Manuals provide the "notes" to be played, but *how* they are played is what conveys therapeutic possibility. It is when the practitioner's relationship to the manual becomes stronger than their relationship to the client that difficulties are most likely to arise.

Models devised for specific problems can be accompanied by a manual requiring strict adherence by the practitioner. The practitioner's compliance with the model is maintained through regular supervision, specifically chosen clients, and a specified, manageable caseload.

The question remains as to how far certain manualised approaches can allow the skill of the practitioner to respond creatively to each unique circumstance. In other words, the question is how far manuals can become HUMANualised. Seasoned practitioners, aware of the need to mould manualised practices to suit their clients, often modify, improvise, discard, pay "lip service", or otherwise adapt their practice according to the complex needs of any given context. They become creatively delinquent. Just as appreciating music involves a complex sensory interplay between participants, so a manual can set the "key" for what is about to be played, but too much direction will lead to a lack of spontaneity.

> A treatment manual contains, "a definitive description of the principles and techniques of [the] psychotherapy ... [and] a clear statement of the operations the therapist is supposed to perform (presenting each technique as concretely as possible ..." (Kessler, 1994, p. 145). (Wampole, 2011, p. 17)

Kessler's quote hints at the practitioner's delinquency when he indicates that the practitioner is *"supposed* to perform". Many practitioners simply do not comply because each practice encounter is unique.

What *is* relevant in using manuals creatively is attention to the mutuality of responsiveness between participants, especially where communal support between clients is a feature of the model. Solidarity and shared care seem powerful ingredients in whether clients make good use of a manualised approach; for example, non-violent resistance (NVR) is a manualised model first developed by Haim Omer in Israel (2004), now widely applied in the UK and elsewhere in Europe. Here, the manual provides a secure set of procedures, activities, and skills which participants find very helpful in changing their responses towards their challenging and violent family member/s. What breathes life into the manual is the skilled way in which participants in the programme connect with each other and the practitioners who assist and teach the model. In this model, parental presence is enhanced, escalation of reactive behaviours between parent and child is reduced, and each participant begins to grasp a sense of their own creative potential to alter their circumstances. Anti-oppressive, democratic processes are embedded in the approach, and help create the conditions for communal resourcefulness and resilience.

In some mental health services, session-by-session forms are used to assess progress, or the lack of it. In certain situations, this could help practitioners and their clients to stay on track. However, reducing the complexity of the client's experience of a session to a number on a piece of paper is a very rough guide, if a guide at all. The idea that the immediate response to a session of, say, fifty minutes, is a gross simplification. It is very difficult for most clients to respond candidly because they might not wish to be impolite, criticise their therapist in case he is offended, or perhaps think they risk being relegated from therapy or seen as obstructive.

A colleague reported to me that one of her clients was handed a service evaluation "postcard" as she left the mental health service. While the session under evaluation had been painful and distressing, it had been sensitively handled. However, the evaluation postcard asked the client to rate the service with "smiley faces", which did not in any way reflect the client's agonies. The client thought that the care offered by the practitioner was excellent but she certainly did not feel like smiling. The evaluation method was described by her as "the kind you get in service stations for rating the cleanliness of public toilets".

When we focus, instead, on practice as a contribution within the multifarious experiences of life outside the therapy room, there is little merit in a "single session" evaluation, any more than one can measure the merits of a single word in a sentence without recourse to the semantic context. Clients leave a session with inner, unspoken responses to what has transpired in the session. They might talk with each other in private about what struck them as important. They might talk with friends and other family members about their experience. They might dream of some connection with the session, and they might rework what they think was important the day after. Or perhaps the session might have become a blur as daily life takes over. So, where really *is* the session, and how is it measured?

Clients might have been given an "experiment" to carry out, or another potentially therapeutic "task", in which case the session was a dry run to experimenting in the world outside. In all this complex process, how can we objectively measure the effect of a fifty-minute or one-hour meeting on the ongoing lives of participants? When reduced to smiley-faced responses, we diminish the therapeutic encounter and, more importantly, the whole psychosocial complexity of the clients' lives, their dealings with our service, and the flow of interaction which can be beyond words, and certainly beyond a tick-box measure. No matter how this could assist, we will only get a momentary temperature reading at one time, in one day in the broad climate changes of the clients' lives.

Ethical concerns

A danger lurks where the selling of a manualised approach tips over into ethical concerns which surface when practitioners are caught in overzealous claims to model effectiveness, and insistence that the model allegiance must prevail at all costs, as the following example illustrates.

The adulterated letter

A practitioner tells me that, while participating within a manualised model prescribed by her agency, she had been working with a parent who composed a therapeutic letter to his son. The father's letter praised his son for making such good progress in his life. It was intended as a mark of recognition for his son's achievement in coming off drugs, and staying out of trouble with the police. The letter was lovingly composed as an intimate message from a father to a son. This matter was later discussed in supervision with the supervisor of the model, who asked for the letter to be sent to him to peruse. Some days passed and when the letter was returned from the supervisor to the practitioner, it had been altered to include praiseworthy comments about the model, and its merits in helping the boy. The adulteration of the letter led the practitioner to resign from the project.

This example illustrates the corruption that can occur when money, brand name, and competition take precedence over honest practice. The example placed the practitioner in the invidious position of being required to comply with the implementation of a model of supervision that directly contradicted her ethics as a professional, and the only option open to her was to leave.

The project continued to receive funding from the local authority concerned because it claimed to be evidence based and effective.

The case of the adulterated letter reveals how power over the practitioner is experienced as oppressive; a deliberate attempt to alter the meaning and purpose of an important therapeutic letter from a father to his son. But more insidious restrictions on ethical practice can occur when practitioners feel their professional autonomy and expression are curtailed by a feeling of being constantly assessed.

In times of uncertainty and insecurity in the health service, there is a push to find certainties that are "cost effective" and rational. Privatisation of large swathes of the National Health Service, social care, and probation service is already under way and this strategy has been gathering apace since the late 1970s. The Health and Social Care Act, 2012, is, "the ultimate act of vandalism in this long funereal recessional from universality" (Davis & Tallis, 2013, p. 203). In this context, strategies to measure goals, outcomes, and effectiveness cannot be disentangled from the political arena within which such initiatives are being implemented.

> The problem extends to how agencies measure productivity ... Agencies frequently experience such economic instability that their driving goal is solvency and survival—thus the intense focus on ... productivity. Regulation, institutionalised habits, management policies, and cost effectiveness measures all tend to reward predictability and the appearance of competency. (Miller & Hubble, 2011, p. 26)

A residential social worker confided in me that he wanted out of residential care work after twenty years because the new system of care in his authority was more concerned with filling beds and getting in cheaper, unqualified staff to run residential homes. He was dismayed; "It's all about money, changing status, and changing values."

Restrictions in mental health provision lead financial commissioners to look for savings that rationalise service delivery, but the consequences for clients and practitioners are frequently not fully appreciated. A false economy results whereby cuts in services lead ultimately to greater demand because of a lack of appropriate response to early signs of distress, especially where frontline, community based, and voluntary sector projects are no longer available to people.

Measurements of service effectiveness are affected by financial interest. Avoiding the most complex social material problems faced by clients allows for the appearance of better outcomes. A recently published report on policing sexual abuse of children in Rotherham (Jay,

2014) revealed that over a third of cases reported were not adequately investigated because police activity was geared up to measure more easily definable statistics about theft and burglary—much easier to investigate and process than following up on the complexity of sexual abuse investigations.

The sociologist Rustin points to the tendency that some practitioners, promoted to higher income bracket management roles, can lose their primary focus on care for the client and, in time, become inducted into the value system of those whose earnings become a more central concern, especially if performance is related to income and there is a fear of losing one's highly paid job. Incentivising managers more often leads to a "displacement of attention from the provision of the service, and the complex systems and cultures required to achieve this, to the short term aims of financial return" (Rustin, 2015, p. 8). He goes on to write,

> It is the same logic which now demands that provider organisations and their sub-units operate as businesses or quasi-businesses with the state of their balance-sheets given priority over all other indicators of their performance and value, (p. 8)

Practitioners might be recruited into such positions where these values are given weight. The idea here is that, in time, the values of commodity before care become the new norm. This "weakens the practitioner's identification with the professional cultures and values in which they often began their careers, and . . . recruit[s] them as accomplices to the new order of the rich" (Rustin, 2015, p. 9).

He describes the process thus:

> . . . what may well begin, for a senior public manager, as an external pressure on him or her to meet demands to achieve greater efficiency or solvency, over time may become an internalised commitment to financial goals. These now come to be perceived as the only reality that matters, in contradistinction to what they may now see as a merely sentimental or reactionary loyalty of more junior organisational members to professional client-oriented goals and methods. (p. 9)

Managers, commissioners, and policy makers are all invested in maintaining practices that will either enhance or limit effectiveness.

Cuts to services mean that decisions are made at a political level by professionals who also feel their hands are tied to operate within restrictions. When this translates into policies that hunt for efficiency savings at the cost of quality of services, dehumanisation in practice can result. When human distress is viewed from the distance of statistical analysis, the danger is in losing sight of the reality of suffering.

The division between businessminded management, and client-centred services creates enormous problems for practitioners and their clients. The more distant the manager is from face-to-face client contact, the more this divorce is likely to occur. Defending services and working within tight budgetary requirements can create moral dilemmas for managers who want to provide excellent services but who are tied by financial constraints to put forward proposals for cuts that go against their principles. One senior clinical leader told me, "I didn't come into this job to make people redundant." He was clearly upset at the way in which staff were being treated but felt impotent to do anything about it.

Sandel (2012) concludes, in his critique of consumerist society, that the market economy has invaded

> family life, friendships, health education citizenship and death . . . once we see that markets and commerce change the character of the goods they touch we have to ask where markets belong—and where they don't. And we can't answer that question without deliberating about the meaning and purpose of goods and the values that surround them . . . What matters is a terrain we sometimes fear to tread. For fear of disagreement we hesitate to bring our moral and spiritual convictions into the public square. (p. 202)

This is what is required of us since, if we do not debate these matters, "markets decide them for us" Sandel (p. 202).

Yet another push: greater surveillance creates the panopticon in the head

While a degree of regulatory process can provide helpful indicators about service provision, in practice the growth of assessment tools and protocols, computerised entries detailing all manner of "must do" data is not only time consuming but also has the unfortunate effect of creating an atmosphere of scrutiny by an unseen eye via the computer screen.

The panopticon was an architectural design for a prison. It was initially developed by the philosopher Jeremy Bentham in the late eighteenth century. The principle of the panopticon was to create the means by which prisoners could be under constant observation. The structure consisted of tiers of prison cells, arranged in a circular design. At the very centre of the circular structure was an observation tower that allowed a few guards to survey many prisoners without their knowing whether they were being watched.

Currently, in social care and health services, most activities show up on a computerised diary. Notes are accessible, activity standards are monitored, and there is a growing number of government "must dos" regarding outcome measures for each practice session. This leads many practitioners to put administrative procedures first to ensure that they are not caught out for not completing all the must dos. Even when not observed, there is the possibility of being observed by the "panopticon" inside the computer. This can create anxiety, and a desire to please the invisible observer. However, the panopticon in the computer can insidiously become the panopticon in the head, and might have the effect of making practitioners more determined to complete form filling to satisfy the observer—whoever he/she is.

One practitioner reported to me that she had been instructed to check up on another colleague's case notes to see if everything was in order. She refused to do this when she was told her colleague had not been informed of this action. Practitioners who refuse to comply are at risk of being seen as oppositional, refusing to do part of the job they are employed to carry out. The temptation is to play safe, yet playing safe creates uncertainty, as though one is not being true to oneself.

One colleague facing complicated changes in her work structure, procedures, and enforced cuts to her service said, "All change is difficult. It's just a matter of learning to get used to the changes." Here, the focus is displaced on to the process of change itself rather than considering a critique of the reasons or consequences of the impending change. "We simply need to adjust", seemed to be the logic. But this response avoids any critical consideration of what is at stake for the service and the personnel.

Practitioners who have the courage to complain about poor, inadequate, or damaging practices, take major risks of being ostracised, or threatened with disciplinary action; documentation of such responses to opening claims of malpractice are recorded regularly in the UK press. Despite policies in support of such "whistle blowing", practitioners might not feel it is safe to lodge complaints and, instead, stay quiet or pretend not to notice.

> ... if the obvious is not of a kind that [the person] can easily assimilate without internal disturbance, their self-corrective mechanisms work to side-track it, to hide it, even to the extent of shutting the eyes if necessary, or shutting off various parts of the process of perception. (Bateson, 1973, p. 405)

Pushing back against the language of social disconnection

"When words are spoken in the open they can become extremely powerful; a fantasy or fiction may start to exist as fact, in time, if it is talked about long enough and is afforded credibility" (Tom Andersen, personal communication).

Pejorative language enters professional discourse when subtlety and complex thinking is reduced. Of course, few colleagues make such overt criticisms of clients, but work stresses can thin out complex understandings and create a myopic vision of the client's predicaments.

The unemployed can be considered "chavs" and scroungers living off the state; patients of mental health services must declare their deficiency before receiving extra financial support. When judged in this light, sensitivity to the plight of the poor is replaced by an attitude of blame. One client told me that when she had to attend for interview to claim her state benefits, she was made to feel she had caused her own life difficulties. In this case, the woman had been living in damp accommodation with four children and striving to get through each day on very little income or support. Her main problems were material, and this material impoverishment had direct effects on her psychological health. However, in case discussion this obvious truth was not addressed; instead her son's supposed ADHD was the focus for treatment.

Jones (2012), in his study into contemporary prejudices about the working class, argues that we are retreating from the politics of class and, instead, are using identity politics to avoid class differences in favour of an individualised description of identity. He suggests that the desire and duty to assist fellow human beings is being replaced by the "atomised, consuming, acquisitive self" (p. 258). We strip away inspirational ideas about communal ways of tackling difficulties and replace them with individualised responses that are limited in their appreciation of wider contextual influences on the client's life. By doing so, we decontextualise the context of the client and see only the isolated individual whose own shortcomings have led to his or her problems in life.

In one mental health team meeting, I asked for the topic of poverty to be discussed as part of the agenda. It was met with surprise, since the bulk of the team business meeting was taken up with a detailed analysis of the various assessment tools and measures that had to be implemented and computerised. This kind of myopia eventually screens out open discussion of the wider vision of practice and the profound importance of social conditions in creating problems of human distress.

The way matters of importance become marginalised by an over focus on the minutiae of procedures is a sobering consideration. How can a systemic humanist approach help in seeing what is possible to counter the commodification and simplification of practices?

Pushing against dehumanising practices

At a recent conference proposing the establishing of a critical psychotherapy movement (May 2014, Anna Freud Centre), the claim was made by several speakers (Lowenthal, 2015) advocating for psychodynamic, and other forms of psychotherapy to be much more inclusive of a socially orientated training and practice. One speaker advocated not just infant observation as part of psychotherapy training, but also placing equal emphasis on trainee therapists' and psychologists' observation of processes within organisations, as well as much more focus in community-based placements in areas of major deprivation and challenge. The claim was made that too many trained therapists opt out of the public services instead of trying to create changes from within.

The psychologist Mair (2014) represents a body of psychology critical of the mechanistic ways in which practitioners in psychology are trained into the language of measurement, or, as one colleague put it, "manualised labour". This critical voice within psychology redresses the mechanistic prerogative of the profession by trying to uphold other perspectives: the poetic, spiritual, and aesthetic. The systemic humanist is not in opposition to the usefulness of scientific enquiry, but against the dehumanisation of practice that objectifies and reduces the complexity of human distress to simplified categories of description. It is important to avoid the false antithesis between the rational and the emotional or between practice as a science or an art:

> ... what we are dealing with here is not a simple duel between feeling and reason—nor one between science and the arts—to be resolved by a victory for one side. We need somehow to value and celebrate scientific knowledge without being dragooned into accepting propaganda which suggests it is the only thing that matters. (Midgley, 2001, pp. 52–53)

When the expression of human distress is reduced by a diagnosis that fails to account for the complexity of a person's life, it becomes like picking "collections of dried flowers drawn from the much richer and wilder woodlands that we call states of mind" (Midgley, 2001 p. 111). Mair, and critical psychologist Smail (1987, 2006), also emphasise the "wild woodlands" of a more communal, relational orientation coupled with a critical view of political interests as they shape practice. (See, for example, the *Social Materialist Manifesto*, 2012.)

Many psychologists require to undertake a training that encompasses the "history and philosophies of knowledge and research to be attained by every qualifying psychologist" (Burns, 2014, p. 34). She argues that all psychologists, in their formulations, "have to integrate our understanding of the internal and external world in terms of psychological explanation" (p. 35), including the importance of systemic conceptualisation in training and practice. This is a strong statement in support of a complex social relational knowledge base to the profession. However, the conditions in which psychologists and practitioners from related disciplines find themselves practising in many agencies, including parts of the NHS, do not allow them to bring their wealth of training to the fore. On the contrary, many practitioners are extremely frustrated at not being able to put their knowledge and skill into practice because the job they are obliged to do simply does not allow time or place for their creativity to find expression.

For creativity in practice to thrive, participants engage in human connectedness that avoids too much religious regard for procedures. Procedures set parameters for practitioners and help focus attention on central matters of concern, but they need to have life breathed into them by listening to the impressions of practitioners, tapping their practice wisdom, and generating useful dialogues that promote sensitive thoughtful decisions. Procedures are best seen as useful guides, not dictators.

Cuts and constraints have an impact on direct practice in processes that, at best, restrict co-creativity and, at worst, lead to dehumanising social relations entwining clients and practitioners in ways of thinking and acting that replicate oppressive practices in the workplace. This chapter has set out to convey the main forces that push practice from behind and describe the ways in which distal forces and political policies have a direct bearing on how practice is measured and assessed and services are reshaped. The implications for maintaining an ethically sound, humanising practice are evident from the foregoing discussion and I summarise here the constraints on expression that can permeate daily practice in many settings, as well as threaten to dehumanise practice.

- How clients are talked about in an objectifying or pathologising way, rather than in a language based on compassion which is cognisant of socio–political understanding of human distress. We are not saints, but when I find myself expressing negative prejudices about a client, I try to convert this negativity into some useful starting point for reflection. We all have prejudices; the point is not to let them remain unexplored or avoided. They can be a source of fresh thinking about mutual systemic influences on interaction (see Burck, 2010; Cecchin et al., 1994).
- How objective assessments fail to consider the subjective experience of the practitioner who is making the assessment. This restricts the practitioner to thinking only about the fit between the problem and the method to be applied, rather than including the fit between the practitioner and the client in a joint relational engagement and collaboration.
- How practice and policies detract from creative expression and collaborative endeavour and, instead, conspire to put a strain on human connection through the imposition of mechanistic measures for meeting targets.

- How organisational policies are driven by through-put of clients at the expense of distancing the practitioner from the specific needs of the client. This creates an ethical dissonance between one's values about what should be done to assist a client and what is determined instead by the "must do" protocols. This contributes to stress in practitioners, and is even worse when they are frightened to speak out about the contradictions between what they believe in and what is demanded of them. The desire to do "things by the book" can, paradoxically, lead to adverse effects in risk assessment. If practitioners are more preoccupied with being seen to follow the correct procedure, they might be at risk of creating an atmosphere of anxiety that is conveyed to the client. Without conditions for considered, reflective thinking, the very attempts to reduce risk can create the opposite effect. Risk-averse practice can increase risk.
- How the apparent priority for the service is one of proving its own effectiveness rather than, and often at the expense of, high quality humanising practice. The worst excesses of this neglect are revealed in cruelty and abuse of clients.
- How and where dehumanisation occurs because of draconian cuts in services through personnel changes, cuts in staffing, and reorganisation of services without satisfactory consultation. The worst excesses of this process are where anxiety about job security, and competition between factions and disciplines erupts. This starves open dialogue replacing it with directives and decisions that are experienced as painfully disregarding of the integrity of each person affected.

Checking in with you

I can imagine that, in reading through the constraints to humanising practice, you might be wondering—so what can be done by me? If I pitch my aims too high, I will lose heart. If I settle for too little, I remain tied to compliance. What is it possible to do to maintain our integrity, provide a humanising service to clients, and see the creative potential in what can be done? The shift from what *I* can do alone to what *we* can do together is an important one. Such shifts in the culture of practice raise many questions for practitioners involved.

Here are some frequently posed questions that workshop participants explore as ways to open discussion towards a communal focus on group resources as a source of inspiration. You might like to take time to explore some of these questions with colleagues to bring the discussion about creativity and constraints more into the open.

- What constrains co-creativity in your work context as result of the cuts in services?
- What ideas about the definition of a client's distress take precedence in the culture of your work context? For example, in what ways are problem definitions dislocated from their social context?
- What happens to you as a practitioner when you are asked to comply with ways of working that contradict your ethical views about doing a good job? To whom do you turn to discuss and act on these contradictions?
- Where are the resources within your team/informal collegiate group/management systems that can provide more opportunities to create contexts of co-creativity?

Threaded through the previous chapters has been a consideration of the constraints to creativity seen through the lens of a systemic humanist orientation to practice. In this chapter, I have focused more attention on the psychosocial and political contexts of challenges set before us as "possibilists" in relation to financial cuts, the increased commodification of services, and the consequent ethical and practical hurdles they erect.

The main point to make is that the challenge of providing a high-quality service is not solved by devising yet more models of practice that ostensibly argue for effective outcomes, yet fail to meet the socially complex contexts of practice in many mental health and social care services. The major thrust for tackling social relational causes of much human distress must lie beyond the horizons of specific modalities that see only part of the landscape. This wider vision moves towards developing a skilled workforce implementing thought through co-ordinated services which place a social relational and politically informed analysis on expressions of human distress. The tendency towards further model manufacturing is pulling services and practitioners away from essential elements in the helping process—matters that have been discussed in the body of the book.

By focusing attention on increasing a skilled workforce with systems of collegiate support and solidarity, models and methods could be usefully adapted so long as time for critical reflection on the unique circumstances of the people we seek to help are uppermost in the mind of the practitioner. The term "multi-modal" may be helpful, but multi-modal practices need to be wedded to a process of humanisation, otherwise practitioners remain technicians and not participants in changing social relational contexts of oppression of which we are also a part. What counts is a system of social care and mental health provision that upholds the will and capacity of skilled practitioners to put in place imaginative, creative, and humanising practices that engage the creativity of the client. This system of care is only feasible when priority is given to providing social care and mental health services that are substantially funded and where recognition is given to the value of communal practices that tap the creativity of the individual in their social relational contexts. The next chapter considers what can be learnt from practitioners on what keeps practice alive and explores the importance of ideals that matter to us all in "keeping on keeping on".

CHAPTER SEVEN

How do we keep on keeping on?

In my career to date, I have worked in local authority social work, the voluntary sector, independent private service provision, and in the National Health Service. Therefore, I have had the opportunity to see from the inside of organisations and their functioning from the perspective of a practitioner as well as from the outside, as visiting consultant trainer, or supervisor. These various positions provide different possibilities to contribute, to challenge, and/or feel the power to comply with, the status quo. As a consultant or visiting lecturer, I can try to contribute from the sidelines, so to speak, as adviser, educator, facilitator, and so on, and to encourage exploratory conversations about matters of ethical importance and creativity. These special settings promote reflection and an opportunity to stand back from the daily pressures and demands of practice.

As a practitioner within an organisation, I am an employee and, therefore, bound by contractual agreement that includes paying me a salary. The organisation calls the tune. I am placed in a relationship to others in my immediate work context who influence, and are influenced by, me. These ongoing social relations in the immediate workplace inform how we conduct our affairs and are shaped by perceived power relations and hierarchical arrangements. I can speak up if I am a consultant more easily than as a practitioner on a short-term contract. If I disagree with an idea a colleague has, I cannot simply walk away as one might do as a visiting trainer. We are caught in the mix of ongoing social relations in a more professionally intimate way. As a visiting lecturer or consultant, I still walk away at the end of the day. So, when we discuss what keeps us going and striving to improve our creativity in practice, my views always need tempering with what is possible in any given context.

So, what keeps us keeping on?

Having been on a companionable journey through this book, the invitation is to return to the question of what it is possible to achieve without compromising professional judgement and ethical responsibilities. For some, this is a tightrope to be walked, while feeling fearful, perhaps, of falling towards resignation and tired compliance on the one side, or overbalancing and being excluded as a marginal voice on the other. So how, where, and when does creativity come to our assistance? The thrust of the book has been to look for co-creative possibilities, in both clinical practice and within the organisations of which you are a part. How, for example, do we raise matters of ethical concern with managers in our services? Campbell and Groenbaek (2006) propose that where conflict arises between parties, it can be the starting point of creative possibilities. But this context relies on a degree of openness towards generative dialogue, as these authors describe.

> Conflicts are a choice we have and they offer possibilities for understanding and reaching into many areas. When we work with people in organisations, problems; and conflicts are the foundation for development; this opens opportunities to create new and energising discourses. On the other hand, when differences are experienced as opposition, one positions oneself and the other person in a fixed "cemented" relationship: you argue and do not listen to the other person's words and thoughts ... There is no longer a dialogue going on but a double monologue—two parallel monologues. (p. 51)

When the other party has interests that are totally in opposition to one's own, and where listening is not possible, then dialogue cannot take place. This theme became evident recently when I presented a workshop on "Constraints and Creativity" to a group of colleagues, some of whom were on commissioning boards for the NHS.

"What are you doing to help commissioners become more aware of your criticisms and act appropriately to your concerns?" asked one disgruntled commissioner. He was seeking to hear alternative views to the effects of service "reconfiguration" or "refreshing of services" and the constraints he experienced in having to somehow deal with the restrictions imposed on his decision-making possibilities. My response to his question was essentially the same as for frontline workers while acknowledging the constraints of those bodies commissioned with the job of allocating funds for limited resources. First, we look for possible moves that might promote useful dialogue rather than avoid or resign ourselves to accepting cuts as inevitable and particularly where cuts produce ethical considerations or conflicts.

Second, we seek those who can assist in pressuring for change, and there are many examples of such means to engage in a wider political arena, as I have argued earlier. Notable among these are pressure groups and political associations vociferously lobbying to preserve service standards referred to earlier (see Davis & Tallis, 2013). Each practitioner and manager must decide for herself just what critical action is possible in the face of dehumanising practices and policies.

At the same time, when matters become too painful to explore, we can be prone to push them away and choose not to look closer at what is causing us distress. This position also needs to be recognised as a way of trying to cope with insurmountable pressures. However, we might also wish to invite the possibility of opening dialogue on the logic of not opening dialogue, to see if new openings might emerge. A colleague who was recently offering a "Reflecting Space" session for staff in a hard-pressed mental health service was met with stony silence by participants who did not wish to discuss their feelings about the impact of the work on them because it was too overwhelming. "Let's keep our heads down" seemed to be the message, but it could also be the beginning of dialogue rather than the door being closed.

Dealing with such ethical issues on a day-to-day basis in our practice is a micro-political act. How we treat one another is an enactment of the values we hold. Our thoughts inform our actions and our actions translate into thoughts in an ongoing recursive "conversation" with the world around us. To take matters into wider, politically active spheres is also a valid expression of values that uphold practice as a process of humanisation.

If we wish to influence practice beyond our proximal, micro-political activities in the workplace, we can begin to consider action that we can take at other levels of context. This is also a choice, and it must be a realistic one that fits with our passions and our capacity to be involved at a macro-political level.

If I fail to find a way to express my views, and act to counter the injustices I have met in my dealings within the mental health field, I would be dulling my ethical sensibilities. When placing his opposition to political policies since the 1980s, the author and playwright Alan Bennett's pithy remark that "One has only to stand still to become a radical" (Interview, Radio 4, October 2016) speaks to a changing political landscape that has moved far away from values that he upholds. Similarly, I consider that the principles of ethical, systemic humanist practices have been covered over by waves of policies and procedures that overly simplify the social and political dimensions of much human distress. Thus, humanising principles for practice are, more than ever, in need of recognition for the riches they contain, like rock pools visible only when the tide recedes.

Personal narratives on keeping on . . .

The themes identified here are summaries condensed from many conversations with colleagues and workshop participants from diverse cultures and work settings. Their responses reflect the range of settings, cultural differences, and professional experiences on how they act in the face of constraints on their creativity. Here, I summarise the main themes which emerge.

Restlessness guides creative action and opposition to dominant ideas

In conversation with Emeritus Professor of Communication, John Shotter (2016), he comments,

> Even when I'd given up the obsessive idea that a theoretical scheme [to explain human behaviour] could be found, I continued to retain the sense that no matter how much one has succeeded, there is always "something more". One suffers a peculiar restlessness in one's body . . . which can act in a precise guiding fashion . . . This can lead to a

sense in oneself that what one is doing is still not right (both politically and especially ethically).

In Shotter's career, he sat in opposition to dominant ideologies within academic psychology that derided his work. Yet, he persisted. He concludes by commenting on the process of creative opposition as

> beginning with what at first is experienced as a personal want or desire, but which then metamorphoses into a need, an aspect of ourselves which becomes part of our identity, a part of who we are. It is not possible to "give up" without ceasing being ourselves . . . which exerts an extremely powerful influence upon us. (Personal communication, November 2016)

Shotter opposed the vested interests within a hierarchy of academia whose dominant, theoretical positions were worn like suits of armour to defend against his radical critique. Instead of dialogue, there were only power plays. Shotter found common ground with therapists and other like-minded academics in order not to be ground down. Like the rest of us, he needed solace and places where his ideas were valued and supported. We all look for this to have the strength to oppose fictions dressed as new facts, new clothes to cover the naked truth that effectiveness in service delivery rests more on well-staffed, well-supported, and well-resourced services within which many models of practice may find a place, but only if there is room for critical reflection and ingenuity in application. In other words, where services ensure the delivery of responsible, humanising practices.

Keep your options open

One consultant psychologist said, "I know there are institutional 'niches' where there is more freedom from constraints than elsewhere. I try to find them and work there . . . I learnt from my father never to trust one job only . . . so, I always try to have two, hoping I could leave one if I start to hate the work in contexts of unhelpful constraint."

The job is important, but it's not my life!

A Dutch family therapist working in an independent psychotherapy service highlighted this theme:

"I always realise that I am a visitor. I aim to be a meaningful visitor, but I will never go with these people on holidays, hold them when they cry in the night, or sit with them at family feasts. My mission is that they have a better life at home; the short relationship with me serves their long relationships at home."

Where do we place our priorities in life? Do we find creativity in activities aside from our job? What are these sustaining activities that we need to balance creativity in the workplace with a life that also satisfies us elsewhere. I recall a period in my career where my life was, through choice, dedicated to bringing up my children and devoted to becoming a better family therapist. It was a single-minded determination that meant many other aspects of life were pushed to one side. This "work–life balance" was probably useful but, at the same time, it made me rather single-minded and, perhaps, to some, over involved in my work. Each choice will exclude others.

Find a home in an orientation and professional collegiate group that welcomes you

One Swedish colleague expressed his concern and lack of belonging within practice contexts in which a positivistic model of mental health was the dominant discourse.

"[The] increase in the number of psychiatric diagnoses in the past forty years . . . placed the systemic, social constructionist movement as an opposing voice to this unhealthy development . . . I get energised by being part of this important movement to present an alternative world view."

Another colleague from an NHS psychology service commented that in her job she had ample support from her managers and professional leads to allow her the freedom to implement new projects.

"I don't have to make proposals to anonymous administrators and wait three months for a reply."

She spoke of the importance of local connections and direct contact with decision makers within her supportive team. Her professional autonomy was not compromised by "must dos". Her team subscribed to an outlook about practice that was explicitly systemic, and openly inclusive of different modalities. In one team meeting I attended, it was clear from the positive atmosphere that the various models of practice being explored (DBT, EFT, DDP, CBT (third wave), CAT IPT, etc.) had created interest and some lively critical debate. It was an atmosphere of inclusivity that seemed to unite the team with a professional lead who was welcoming of diversity and supportive of the staff group.

Emphasise the artistry in practice and its fascination

Alongside the desire and benefits that stem from being a member of a supportive organisation or team is the fulfilment many colleagues reported in being able to teach and supervise others. This kept alive their critical thinking and ability to see their practice as having the capacity for artistry rather than being defeated by all the protocols that threaten time for reflective creative practice. In my own career, the balance between passionate disagreement with certain ways of treating clients and fellow colleagues in the NHS or elsewhere has been tempered by a desire not to locate the problem inside an individual but to try, wherever possible, to contextualise a matter, to find those resourceful others to develop an argument, and see where there might be cracks in the edifice of bureaucracy that can let in some new light. Artistry lies in doing what is possible, not what is compliant.

One British mental health practitioner said that her orientation to practice was in line with systemic humanism; she was fascinated and intrigued by her practice with children with complex needs, which involved her in multi-level negotiations with many different agencies. This instance highlights the fact that we each have different fascinations and curiosities that, if we are fortunate, can be matched with the areas of practice we desire. The community worker, the nurse therapist, the doctor, and the teacher may express their practice as a process of humanisation in their domains—domains that fascinate them intellectually and allow them to feel they matter.

It's not so much a job, it's more of a vocation

Vocation is concerned with our fitness for our career, and becomes a large part of our identity. This dimension of practice is, for some, a reason to dedicate oneself to serving others despite constraints placed in the way. One Norwegian psychotherapist states:

> "After thirty years as a psychologist and psychotherapist, I am an optimist and I like people more today than when I started out."

The same practitioner comments that, in taking time out from practice after such a long period, he realised that,

> "Something is missing. I have lost something that is part of me. . . . The experience of always being in contact with people who struggle, at the same time showing courage, stamina, and innovation in finding ways of living that include both living with mental suffering, struggle, and challenge and finding ways, and living in, manners that reduce and abolish such experiences."

Some clinicians spoke of religious values embedded in their early family life that acted as a guide to how to conduct their lives in personal and professional domains. This value base seemed to act as a guide to their practice, so that no matter what constraints they faced, they held on to powerful, centrally guiding moral values that helped them to withstand whatever organisational demands were placed upon them. Even so, the balance between experiencing oppression and standing up for what one believes in is not simply down to the moral strength of the individual.

Aim towards innovation and development, despite resource limitations

I recently presented workshops on "Creativity and Constraints" in the Czech Republic. Here, colleagues rejoiced in the freedom they experience in practice to find new, open, and co-operative ways to develop services in therapy and mental health provision that offered a wide horizon of possibility, despite limited access to financial support. Their sense of freedom from past repressive political regimes meant that their valuing of greater openness in communication sat alongside the lack of infrastructural and organisational support. These enthusiastic practitioners kept their optimism alive because they were developing something that was much richer than what had gone before. In their eyes, they were growing new services from the previously barren soil of political repression. At the same time, they recognised the effects of constraints on opportunities to continue to pursue creativity in the face of financial restrictions and limited budgets. Many conducted their therapy as a private enterprise and offered free time to work for NGOs, or other community-based services.

Similarly, in Greece, despite the austerity imposed upon their country's economy, I am regularly in touch with colleagues who are continuing to pursue humanising mental health practices with dedication. The colleagues in Prague, Brno, and Thessaloniki all experience the profound effects of financial constraints and commodification on the quality of their services. We are on common ground and, despite our different cultural histories, we share concern in the provision of services that humanise practice.

From Sao Paulo, Brazil, a university lecturer and practising clinical psychologist wrote to me recently to say,

> "The university is suffering a lot with cutting funds to research. It's a state university so it's suffering very hard with all this. But you know people are great! The students have such strength! Teachers also. We are working in very difficult conditions sometimes, but we do good work despite all of this. I go out of it stimulated by the relations we can have, and with the mobilisation of students and teachers that go on with the projects the best they can."

The resurgence of one UK child and family psychology service took place following a period of restrictions and lack of support felt by service leaders. They described how "swimming against the tide" made them stronger. Their perseverance was almost exhausted when, at last, new managers of the service began to support their vision of the future of family psychology in the region. Their vision found support within the organisation hierarchy, and at that point the sense of oppression stopped. They recalled how important it was to state what they believed in without compromise, and knew that if their vision were not recognised, they would leave the service. They described the moment when they faced a major confrontation with service managers as a tipping point. Had the new direction not been offered to de-escalate the growing frustration and oppression of the team, the team leaders would have left. This example shows how necessary it is for keen negotiation skills to be developed in arguing for sustainable services, but it also addresses the need for dialogue between levels of management and practitioner to be open and collegiate. Without the new system of supportive management, the service would probably have seen the resignation of very experienced psychologists.

From stance to circumstance

As the above themes and cultural comparisons suggest, we can, and do, shift our positions with changing circumstance. Practitioners may find new openings in their career, fresh enthusiasm for the job, a new team leader who inspires, and a client group with whom one feels empathy. We respond as life comes to us with opportunities and restrictions that alter our opinions about what to think and do.

In recent workshops with various NHS practitioners in mental health, I have noted the range of responses from despair to enthusiastic determination regarding changes within the NHS, and one key characteristic separates those demoralised by the changes from those who are riding the waves and remain energised: it is, quite simply, solidarity between team members with a shared supportive vision, and a sensitive and savvy management taking care to protect professionalism. There is no short-cut to sensitively delivered services.

The personal is (micro-) political

Our every action is meant as a contribution towards humanisation in practice. When I ignore or denigrate another person, I fall short of this aim; when I listen only to move swiftly on to the next case, I fall short of my ideal. This is a natural failing, otherwise we would not be human; we would be saints. But the point is to value our ideals and recognise the unavoidable struggle to live up to them.

Systemic humanism is an orientation that is expressed in mutual and relational enrichment, characterised by care, advice, and protection, all qualities that sustain relationships and help us to grow. We show these qualities in the day-to-day interaction with others. I recently offered a seminar in Belgrade on "Humanising Practices in Child Mental Health". The young men in the audience spoke with me afterwards to say how they had not experienced my teaching style in their studies and training before. It was more open and conversational than they had been used to. They were watching *how* I taught and *how* I responded to questions. The content of the seminar was relevant for their blossoming practice, but the young men were more interested in my manner of address in the way I tried to connect with them. We express our values in the fine detail of the ways we meet with another person. The significance of the small important gestures in meeting with another is expressed by Nietzsche:

> Among the small but endlessly abundant and therefore very effective things that science ought to heed more than the great, rare things, is goodwill ... I mean those expressions of a friendly disposition in interactions; that smile of the eye, those handclasps, and the ease which usually envelops nearly all human actions. Every teacher ... brings this ingredient to what he considers his duty. It is the continual manifestation of our humanity, its rays of light, so to speak in which everything grows ... Good nature, friendliness, and courtesy of heart ... have made much greater contributions to culture than those much more famous expressions of this drive, called pity, charity and self-sacrifice. (Nietzsche, cited in Bakewell, 2011, p. 171)

It is this way of trying to be in relation to others that is under attack.

The personal is also (macro) political

Magical consciousness defined by Freire is a form of fatalism that says, in effect, that, "I cannot alter anything because my position in society is where I belong". It is a pernicious view heard where people resign themselves to their place in life as a sufferer or as a compliant figure, ingratiating him or herself with those in power to extract their beneficence.

Domestication of one's vision of life occurs when we are caught in a "circle of certainty" (Freire, 1996, p. 21) accepting the status quo, not challenging events that make us fear taking a risk. Translated into practices in social, educational, and mental health settings, "domestication" is revealed in passivity and compliance, where curiosity is truncated and the practitioner is subsumed in processes which hamper any freedom or adventure in the work.

The opposite of domestication is a form of freedom to experiment; to value joint exploration knowing that, as human beings, we are incomplete and able to become more than we are right now.

This incompleteness implies for us a permanent movement of search. In fact, it would be a contradiction if we who are aware of our incompleteness were not involved in a movement of constant search. For this reason, women and men by the mere fact of being in the world is also necessarily being with the world. Our being is *being with*. So, to be in the world without making history, without being made by it, without creating culture, without a sensibility toward one's own presence in the world, without a dream, without a song, music or painting, without caring for the earth or the water ... without awe in the face of mystery, without learning, instruction, teaching, without ideas on education without being political is a total impossibility. (Freire, 2001, pp. 57–58)

Beginning to see beyond individual oppression is an important step. This can be seen in the example of Sally and her son, David, whom we have met from time to time in this book. Sally began to realise that she had the capacity to change her ways of responding to her son and, in time, altered her own outlook on life as a more assertive, outgoing woman. Freire would call this the shift from a naïve consciousness (seeing oneself at fault) towards a transformation of her situation, combining resources and creativity to assist her life and that of others. This is transformation in relational life, not simply in ways of thinking.

Dehumanisation is systemic

Many of the constraints I have discussed have been experienced by me in my practice, and by many of my colleagues in different social care and mental health settings in recent years. The question facing us is how to carry on and continue to hold a critical voice against practices that confine practitioners and their clients to services that fall short of our ethical values as to what is needed to help someone in distress. To do this, we need to have a grasp of what we believe in, and ideals to try to pursue a better way of practising our craft. This extract from a speech by actor Michael Sheen at the St David's Day celebration of the NHS on 1 March 2015 expresses it well.

> ... [D]o we want a society where each person is recognised? Where all are equal in worth and value. And where that value is not purely a

monetary one. A society that is supportive, that is inclusive and compassionate. Where it is acknowledged that not all can prosper, where those who are most vulnerable, most in need of help, are not seen as lazy, or scrounging, or robbing the rest of us for whatever they can get. Where we . . . do not turn our backs on [them] . . . [b]ecause they are us. (Sheen, 2015)

The passion in Sheen's speech is a call for a relationally focused society: "attentive to the developments and needs of others as well as to their own interests . . . more relevant to human wellbeing than the pursuit of the chimera of 'economic growth' as the measure of human happiness" (Rustin, 2015, p. 16).

A desire to change a monetarised climate of relating to service requires more than a token gesture towards good practice. If everything has a market value, and can be branded, we would need to guard against humanising practices similarly becoming packaged and domesticated: "stolen by management personnel and customer relations departments to make it seem as if their organisations have become more sensitive to human needs, while in reality little has been altered but appearances", warns Rustin (2015, p. 14).

To sustain a relationally focused service requires well-trained, conscientious personnel in sufficient numbers to meet client need. Given that the key factors in good therapeutic outcome are the four "Cs" identified by Gawande as: care, consistency, conscientiousness, and commitment, we should be mindful of not replacing the four Cs by the four "Ms", monetarism, manualisation, marketisation, and marginalisation, that cut into the fabric of care for both the client and the practitioner trying to help.

Forms of accountability in services that are routine are "engines of standardisation" (Rustin, 2015, p. 15) and should be replaced by feedback-informed practices where the client's experience is central to the practitioner's measure of direction. Specifically, the shift in emphasis from accountability, with its connotations of blame and imposition, should be towards responsibility which emphasises, instead, the process of atonement between client and practitioner, a focus on outcome that is directly related to the development of the therapeutic alliance and constant dedication to responsive interaction and detailed attention to the unique experience of the encounter between client and therapist.

Practitioners who have been through inspections in social care, education and mental health services fear—quite naturally—being caught out, not because they have been negligent, but because this is a normal response when practitioners are keen to do a good job. Everybody makes mistakes. The biggest mistake arises when these are covered up by equally fearful managers who are afraid of disciplinary action against the service. In this scenario, each person feels oppressed, whether manager or practitioner. In all this fearfulness about what to do, it is hardly surprising that creativity suffers. We need to own up to mistakes, and share them with others to learn without further fear of litigation. There is no fail-safe way to work with patients and clients.

Drawing attention to aspects of practice that dehumanise patients is also to address the dehumanisation of staff who carry out such bad practices. This is further compounded if those who address dehumanising practices are themselves vilified. Davis and Tallis (2013) refers to the Francis Report, which identified the vilification of whistle blowers who subsequently found it difficult to find jobs within the NHS. This fear of addressing bad practice led doctors to remain silent in the

> face of wholesale abuse of patients in the Mid Staffordshire NHS Foundation Trust. The Department of Health has spent very large sums of money on "gagging agreements" for individuals dismissed from the service. A "culture more of fear and of compliance than of learning, innovation and enthusiastic participation in improvement" was identified in a report commissioned from Joint Commission International. (Davis & Tallis, 2013, p. 8)

Reflection: an exercise exploring the things that matter to you

Our relationship to risk taking, challenge, compliance, and our motivation to do the job we do are brought to us in the various colleagues' narratives. The circumstances that shape how we "keep on keeping on" are varied and seem to centre around the values that fuel our perseverance and continued commitment to find ways to remain creative in humanising practices. These values may be described as finding their foundations in aspects of our family scripts (Byng-Hall, 1996).

For some, the ethical struggles in practice create friction of tectonic proportions, while for others this disjunction is not felt so keenly. The following exercise might be useful to you in exploring the themes further in your setting with trusted colleagues.

Chapter Three concluded with an exercise with two of your colleagues in exploring your relationship to your creativity. A similarly structured exercise can also help us to look in more detail at our relationship to the values we hold. I have used the "Relationship with Values" exercise in training and workshop contexts; participants often find that the time taken to do the exercise (about one hour) helps transcend all the "must do" constraints by focusing on what practitioners hold as deeply held personal values that are relevant and necessary in the jobs we do. If you should decide to do this exercise with two colleagues, the most straightforward way to proceed is to substitute the character, "Your Values" for the character of "Your Creativity", as in the earlier exercise. The sequence remains the same: first, focus on how your values are currently expressed and find satisfaction in the job you do. Second, think of how your core values are challenged and constrained, and last, how to embed your values even more in your practice. Just as before, the exercise is repeated so each participant has a chance to present his or her values for exploration.

Keeping on . . .

"A change in the human heart is possible only to the extent that drastic economic and social changes occur that give the human heart the chance for change and the courage and vision to achieve it" (Fromm, 1997, p. 8).

Systemic humanism places a social relational focus on practice and the practitioner. It is embedded in a socio–political critique of practices, especially those practices that threaten, or act in opposition to, systemic humanism, as described in these pages. A systemic humanist orientation brings into critical focus those policies and organisational processes which many practitioners are concerned about. We cannot limit our thinking only to what happens when we meet our clients in a therapy session. The constraints and anxieties experienced by practitioners inform the service our clients receive. The clinical therapy room is only one context in which systemic humanising values are enacted. How we treat our clients, and how we attend to one another in humanising ways, involves learning from each other and being enriched by the meeting in whatever context we participate.

I have aimed to offer you companionship in exploring themes that are pertinent to practitioners, themes that are troubling many who feel dissatisfied with the way services are increasingly being delivered with a purely commercial business ethos.

If political expression only offers strident criticism without creative action, it becomes tiresome rhetoric. I believe we need a combination of humility and creative opposition to dehumanisation, in practice as in life. The first step is to discuss the stresses and dissatisfactions, the injustices, and the desire for something better. This is a big step. The second step is to find creative, ethically congruent ways to act so that our steps, no matter how small or faltering, can allow us to feel that we recognise ourselves in the jobs we do.

In this book, we have met with many clients and their resourcefulness, their ability to face up to personal and situational constraints, and still find creativity to tackle and overcome problems in their lives.

The transformations of Sally and her son, the "fearful woman", the family that was willing to experiment with playback therapy, and all the other clients who have featured in these pages are offered here for your companionship, and, one hopes, inspiration.

> The pursuit of full humanity cannot be carried out in isolation or individualism, but only in fellowship and solidarity; therefore, it cannot unfold in the antagonistic relations between oppressors and oppressed. No one can be authentically human while he prevents others from being so. (Freire, 1996, p. 66)

Since dehumanisation is a systemic process, we are unavoidably part of a context that has a deep and lasting effect on all of us unless we bring words and actions to oppose what we see as dehumanising. To do this in isolation is impossible, but to work with others, in whatever form, *is* possible. To echo the father in the playback therapy session, "Now I've seen you portray my family . . . I don't feel so alone."

By drawing attention to the micro- and macro-political actions of practitioners' activity, I also argue that our client's actions and values are similarly structured in response to a political system that has a profound impact on how we value one another. Focusing on the emergent possibilities between us in creating a therapeutic alliance is mutually enriching. The opposite direction is also possible if we are tied to must dos that limit expression of what might be achieved.

Our knowledge of the complexity of practice is never closed. It emerges "only through invention and re-invention, through the restless, impatient continuing hopeful enquiry human beings pursue in the world, with the world and each other" (Freire, 1996, p. 53).

For over thirty years, I have practised as a social worker and family/systemic therapist. I have been fortunate to find colleagues and reference groups that have made me feel at home in their company. Without this sense of professional belongingness, I would have lost heart. The creative edge of practice is to remain irreverent, dissident, and an experimentalist. Opposition towards any prescribed, dictatorial, and dehumanising ways of treating one another is the fire in the belly that needs expression. No one can dictate how you respond to injustices, poor services, and dehumanising practices, but it is important to bring these matters into debate, to face up to what we see and say what we do not see. To seek for the psychosocial resources in practice is a guiding principle that does not avoid attention to the pain of people in distress. It reaches towards what creative possibilities can be developed; it holds on to ideals while remaining a "possibilist". In this context, the reaching for what is just out of our grasp keeps me going. I hope this book has allowed you to "keep on keeping on", finding companionship in your practice and your life.

EPILOGUE

The journey home

From the top of Shooters Hill I can see the Shard shafting the sky above London. It has been a good day. Most of the families and young people turned up for their appointments. My notes are more or less up to date. I am tired but I have been totally absorbed in the work of the last nine hours. The bus arrives and I sit beside a young colleague who has a two-hour commute home.

"Busy day . . . as usual?" I enquire.

She nods enthusiastically.

I am glad to be part of a profession that has such committed, good-hearted people in its midst. We talk about the latest goal-setting regulation shortly to be introduced. I sigh, "More of the same."

She says, "Yeah, that's the way it goes. How is the book coming along?"

"Oh, not bad", I say. "Thought I might start with a journey into work . . ."

Later, I am listening on my iPod to John Martyn singing,

> May you never lay your head down without a hand to hold.
> May you never make your bed out in the cold . . .

We all need companions . . .

I ponder these words as I look out of the window, passing Woolwich Barracks. All is quiet.

NOTE

1. The term "prejudice" is used here as an aid to thinking in practices whereby our prejudices (strong biases) are actively addressed to help appreciate the interaction with others and their biases. Interaction is shaped by the interplay of each participant's prejudices of one sort or another; examining closely our own ideas and how they affect interaction is a core concept in the work of Cecchin, Lane, and Ray.

REFERENCES

Afuape, T. (2011). *Power, Resistance and Liberation in Therapy with Survivors of Trauma: To Have our Hearts Broken*. London: Routledge.
Andersen, T. (Ed.) (1990). *The Reflecting Team*. New York: Norton.
Anderson, H. (1997). *Conversation, Language and Possibilities: A Postmodern Approach*. New York: Basic Books.
Bakewell, S. (2011). *How to Live: A Life of Montaigne in One Question and Twenty Attempts*. London: Vintage Books.
Barrett, F. J. (2012). *Yes to the Mess*. Boston, MA: Harvard Business Review Press.
Bateson, G. (1973). *Steps to an Ecology of Mind*. London: Paladin.
Bateson, N. (2016). *Small Arcs of Larger Circles: Framing Through Other Patterns*. Axminster, Devon: Triarchy Press.
Bennett, A. (2006). *Writing Home*. London: Faber and Faber.
Bevan, A. (1952). *In Place of Fear*. New York: Simon & Schuster.
Bownas, J., & Fredman, G. (Eds.) (2017). *Working with Embodiment in Supervision: A Systemic Approach*. London: Routledge.
Burck, C. (2010). From hazardous to collaborative learning: thinking systemically about live supervision group processes. In: C. Burck & G. Daniel (Eds.), *Mirrors and Reflections; Processes of Systemic Supervision* (pp. 141–162). London: Karnac.

Burck, C., & Daniel, G. (Eds.) (2010). *Mirrors and Reflections: Processes of Systemic Supervision*. London: Karnac.

Burns, J. (2014). A response: a political–representational crisis. *Clinical Psychology Forum, 256*: 30–34.

Byng-Hall, J. (1996). *Rewriting Family Scripts*. New York: Guilford Press.

Byrne, N., & McCarthy, I. (2007). The dialectical structure of hope and despair: a fifth province approach. In: *Hope and Despair in Narrative and Family Therapy: Adversity, Forgiveness and Reconciliation* (pp. 36–48). London: Routledge.

Campbell, D., & Groenbaek, M. (2006). *Taking Positions in the Organization*. London: Karnac.

Cecchin, G. (1987). Hypothesising, circularity and neutrality revisited: an invitation to curiosity. *Family Process, 26*: 405–413.

Cecchin, G., Lane, G., & Ray, W. A. (1992). *Irreverence: A Strategy for Therapists' Survival*. London: Karnac.

Cecchin, G., Lane, G., & Ray, W. A. (1994). *The Cybernetics of Prejudices in the Practice of Psychotherapy*. London: Karnac.

Collins Latin Dictionary and Grammar (1997). London: HarperCollins.

Davis, J., & Tallis, R. (Eds.) (2013). *NHS. SOS*. London: Oneworld.

De Montaigne, M. (2004). *The Essays: A Selection*. London: Penguin.

Equality Trust (2016). Inequality is not inevitable: our new guide for activists. December. Accessed at: www.equalitytrust.org.uk/inequality-not-inevitable-our-new-guide-activists.

Fisch, R., Weakland, J., & Segal, L. (1982). *The Tactics of Change: Doing Therapy Briefly*. San Francisco, CA: Jossey–Bass.

Flaskas, C. (2007). The balance of hope and hopelessness. In: C. Flaskas, I. McCarthy, & J. Sheehan (Eds.), *Hope and Despair in Narrative and Family Therapy: Adversity, Forgiveness and Reconciliation* (pp. 24–35). London: Routledge.

Freire, P. (1996). *Pedagogy of the Oppressed*. London: Penguin.

Freire, P. (1998). *Pedagogy of Freedom*. New York: Rowman & Littlefield.

Fromm, E. (1964). *The Heart of Man; Its Genius for Good and Evil*. New York: AMHF.

Fromm, E. (1981). *On Disobedience: Why Freedom Means Saying "No" to Power*. New York: Harper Perennial.

Fromm, E. (1997). *To Have or To Be*. London: Bloomsbury.

Gawande, A. (2014). Reith Lecture: The idea of wellbeing. BBC broadcast, 20 December 2014.

Gawande, A. (2015). *Being Mortal: Illness, Medicine, and What Matters in the End*. London: Wellcome Collection.

Gergen, K. J. (2009). *Relational Being: Beyond Self and Community.* Oxford: Oxford University Press.
Havel, V. (1991). *Disturbing the Peace.* New York: Vintage.
Heimann, C. (2009). *Guardian* guide to performance. 9 May: Guardian News and Media.
Hodgkinson, W. (2006). *Guitar Man.* London: Bloomsbury.
Hoffman, L. (2002). *Family Therapy: An Intimate History.* New York: W. W. Norton.
Holzman, L. (2009). *Vygotsky at Work and* Play. London. New York: Routledge.
Jay, A. (2014). *Independent Inquiry into Child Sexual Exploitation. Rotherham, 1997–2013.* Rotherham: Rotherham Metropolitan Borough Council.
Jones, O. (2012). *Chavs: The Demonization of the Working Class.* London: Verso.
Keeney, B. (1992). Foreword. In: G. Cecchin, G. Lane, & W. A. Ray (Eds.), *Irreverence: A Strategy for Therapists' Survival* (pp. ix–xi). London: Karnac.
Keeney, B. (2009). *The Creative Therapist: The Art of Awakening a Session.* New York: Routledge.
Knoblauch, S. H. (2000). *The Musical Edge of Therapeutic Dialogue.* Hillsdale, NJ: Analytic Press.
Lowenthal, D. (Ed.) (2015). *Critical Psychotherapy, Psychoanalysis and Counselling.* London: Palgrave Macmillan.
Mair, M. (2014). *Another Way of Knowing: The Poetry of Psychological Inquiry.* Blackrock Co. Dublin: Raven Books.
Marsh, H. (2014). *Do No Harm: Stories of Life, Death and Brain Surgery.* London: Weidenfeld & Nicolson.
Mason, B. (1993). Towards positions of safe uncertainty. *Human Systems*, 4: 189–200.
McCarthy, I., & Byrne, N. (2008). A fifth province approach to intra-cultural issues in an Irish context: marginal illuminations. In: M. McGoldrick & K. Hardy (Eds.), *Revisioning Family Therapy: Race, Class, Culture and Gender in Clinical Practice* (2nd edn) (pp. 327–343). New York: Guilford Press.
Midgley, M. (2001). *Science and Poetry.* London: Routledge.
Miller, S., & Hubble, M. (2011). The road to mastery. *Psychotherapy Networker* (May/June): 22–31, 60.
Montouri, A. (2005). Gregory Bateson and the promise of transdisciplinarity. *Cybernetics and Human Knowing*, 12: 1–2: 147–158.

Montouri, A., & Purser, R. E. (2000). In search of creativity: beyond individualism and collectivism. "Work in progress", Western Academy of Management Conference, Hawaii, March.

Omer, H. (2004). *Non Violent Resistance: a New Approach to Violent and Self-destructive Children*. New York: Cambridge University Press.

Palmer, R. E. (Ed) (2001). *Gadamer in Conversation*. New York: Yale University Press.

Partridge, K. (2010). Systemic supervision in agency contexts: an evolving conversation with clinical psychologists in a mental health trust. In: C. Burck & C. Daniel (Eds.), *Mirrors and Reflections: Processes of Systemic Supervision* (pp. 309–336). London: Karnac.

Phillips, A., & Taylor, B. (2009). *On Kindness*. London: Penguin.

Prigogine, I., & Stengers, I. (1984). *Order out of Chaos*. New York: Bantam.

Rober, P. (2017). *In Therapy Together: Family Therapy as a Dialogue*. London: Palgrave.

Robinson, K. (2001). *Out of Our Minds: Learning To Be Creative*. Oxford: Capstone.

Rustin, M. (2015). A relational society. In: S. Hall, D. Massey, & M. Rustin (Eds.), *After Neoliberalism? The Kilburn Manifesto* (pp. 37–51). London: Lawrence & Wishart.

Salamon, E., & McCarthy, I. (2016). Hope and risk: systemic practices for supervision and assessment in child protection. In: I. McCarthy & G. Simon (Eds.), *Systemic Therapy as Transformative Practice* (pp. 284–297). Farnhill: Everything is Connected Press.

Samuels, A. (2015). Everything you always wanted to know about therapy (but were afraid to ask): fragments of a critical psychotherapy. In: D. Lowenthal (Ed.), *Critical Psychotherapy, Psychoanalysis and Counselling* (pp. 159–174). London: Palgrave Macmillan.

Sandel, M. (2012). *What Money Can't Buy*. London: Allan Lane.

Schon, D. A. (1986). *The Reflective Practitioner: How Professionals Think in Action*. New York: Basic Books.

Seikkula, J., & Arnkil, T. E. (2014). *Open Dialogues and Anticipations: Respecting Otherness in the Present Moment*. Tampere: National Institute for Health and Welfare.

Sheen, M. (2015). By God, believe in something. Transcript of speech in celebration of the NHS. *Guardian*, 2 March.

Shepherd, R., Johns, J., & Taylor Robinson, H. (Eds.) (1996). *D. W. Winnicott: Thinking About Children*. London: Karnac.

Shotter, J. (2016). *Speaking Actually, Towards a New 'Fluid' Common–Sense; Understanding of Relational Becomings*. Farnhill: Everything is Connected Press.

Simon, G., & Chard, A. (Eds.) (2014). *Systemic Inquiry; Innovations in Reflexive Practice Research*. Farnhill: Everything is Connected Press.

Smail, D. (1987). *Taking Care: An Alternative to Therapy*. London: Dent.

Smail, D. (2006). *Power, Interest and Psychology*. Ross–on–Wye: PCCS Books.

Social Materialist Manifesto (2012). *Journal of Critical Psychology, Counselling & Psychotherapy*, 12(2): 93–107.

Stephens, J. (1978). *The Crock of Gold*. London: Pan.

Stern, D. N. (2004). *The Present Moment in Psychotherapy and Everyday Life*. New York: W. W. Norton.

Stierlin, H. (1983). Family therapy—a science or an art? *Family Process*, 22(4): 413–423.

Stratton, P. (2016). *The Evidence Base of Family Therapy and Systemic Practice*. London: Association for Family Therapy.

Sundet, R. (2012). Therapist perspectives on the use of feedback on process and outcome: patient–focused research in practice. *Canadian Psychology*, 53(2): 122–130.

Sundet, R. (2014). Patient–focused research supported practices in an intensive family therapy unit. *Journal of Family Therapy*, 36(2): 195–216.

Tallis, R. (2012). *In Defence of Wonder and Other Philosophical Reflections*. Durham: Acumen.

Verheugt-Pleiter, A. J. E., Zevalkink, J., & Schmeets, M. G. J. (Eds.) (2008). *Mentalizing in Child Therapy: Guidelines for Clinical Practitioners*. London: Karnac.

Walrond-Skinner, S. (1976). *Family Therapy: The Treatment of Natural Systems*. London: Routledge & Kegan Paul.

Wampold, B. E. (2011). *The Great Psychotherapy Debate; Models, Methods and Findings*. Hillsdale, NJ: Lawrence Erlbaum.

Watzlawick, P., Weakland, J. H., & Fisch, R. (1974). *Change: Principles of Problem Formation and Problem Resolution*. New York: Norton.

White, M., & Epston, D. (1990). *Narrative Means to Therapeutic Ends*. New York: W. W. Norton.

Wilson, J. (1998). *Child Focused Practice: A Systemic Collaborative Approach*. London: Karnac.

Wilson, J. (2007). *The Performance of Practice; Enhancing the Repertoire of Therapy with Children and Families*. London: Karnac.

Wilson, J. (2013). A social relational critique of the biomedical definition and treatment of ADHD: ethical practical and political implications. *Journal of Family Therapy*, 3: 198–218.

Wilson, J. (2015). Family therapy as a process of humanisation: the contribution and creativity of dialogism. *Australian and New Zealand Journal of Family Therapy*, 36: 6–19.

Wilson, J. (2016). Engaging children and young people: a theatre of possibilities. In: *Narrative Therapies with Children and their Families: A Practitioner's Guide to Concepts and Approaches* (2nd edn) (pp. 91–111). London: Routledge.

INDEX

abuse, 10, 120, 133, 150
   childhood, 7, 112
   emotional, 43
   sexual, 44, 125–126
Afuape, T., 50, 52
Andersen, T., xxx, 46, 67, 129
Anderson, H., 90
anger, xix, 10–11, 15, 48, 71–72, 93, 110, 119
anxiety, xii, xxv, xxviii, 10–11, 13, 31–32, 34, 43, 47, 64, 85, 89, 98, 107, 110, 118–119, 128, 133, 151
Arnkil, T. E., 41, 67, 118

Bakewell, S., 43, 147
Barrett, F. J., 40
Bateson, G., 28, 129
Bateson, N., xvii
behaviour(al), 7, 19, 21, 32, 40, 65
   child's, 76
   cognitive, 78
   communicative, 6
   dismissive, 65
   existing, xxxii
   human, 140
   orientated, xv
   predictable, 74
   problems, 42, 118
   reactive, 122
   risky, 31
   threatening, 72
   troubling, 69
   worrying, 30
Bennett, A., 53, 140
Bentham, J., 128
Bevan, A., 120
Bownas, J., 97
Burck, C., 98, 132
Burns, J., 6, 131
Byng-Hall, J., 150
Byrne, N., xxii, 17

Campbell, D., 16, 138
case studies
   Alan, 85–88
   Anneka, 110

Bill, Jane, and *Tim*, 30–31
David, 17–24, 148
Jane, 10–11
Jenny, 107–108
Jess, Olivia, Sarah, Pete, and *Terry*, 70–71
Mr Harvey, 47–49
Mr Smith, 71–72
Nadir and *Adem*, 88–90
Richard and *Paul*, 93–95, 97
Sally, 18–24, 35, 148, 152
Simone, 69–70
Tim, 118–120
Cecchin, G., xviii, 4, 40, 42, 45, 49, 73–75, 132, 157
Chard, A., 118
Child and Adolescent Mental Health Team (CAMHS), 47, 62
Clapton, E., 45
Cohen, L., xx
Collins Latin Dictionary and Grammar, 49
conflict, xiii, xxii, 28, 70, 103, 138–139
conscious(ness), 43–44, 47, 60
  artistic un-, 84
  creative un-, 84
  critical, 3, 80
  effort, 2
  magical, 147
  naïve, 148

Daniel, G., 98
Davis, J., 125, 139, 150
De Montaigne, M., xxvii
dehumanisation, xxiii, 13, 29, 127, 131, 133, 148, 150, 152
depression, 18–20, 22, 88, 93, 98, 106, 119

El Saadawi, N., xxx–xxxi, 15, 50
Epston, D., 105
Equality Trust, xxiii

Fisch, R., 37
Flaskas, C., 17
Fredman, G., 97

Freire, P., xii, xvi–xvii, xxxi, 1–3, 9, 11, 13, 43, 50, 59, 63, 66, 75, 91, 98, 147–148, 152–153
Fromm, E., 36, 75, 115, 151

Gawande, A., 61, 67, 149
Gergen, K. J., 33
Groenbaek, M., 16, 138
Guthrie, W., 52

Havel, V., 16
Health and Social Care Act, 2012, 125
Heimann, C., 29
Hodgkinson, W., 39
Hoffman, L., 66
Holzman, L., 59
Hubble, M., 44, 125

Jay, A., 125–126
Johns, J., 7
Jones, O., 129

Keeney, B., 74, 109
Knoblauch, S. H., 72–73

Lane, G., xviii, 4, 42, 73–74, 132, 157
listening, 54, 56, 59–62, 64, 66–67, 69–70, 72–73, 79–80, 105, 132, 138
  attentive, 60–61
  complexity of, 68
  creative, 81
  effective, 80
  irreverent, 74–75
  modes of, 66
  sensitive, 60
  silently, 66
  sympathetic, 69
Lowenthal, D., 130

Mair, M., 130–131
Marsh, H., 16, 34
Mason, B., 66
McCarthy, I., xxii, 17, 112
Metropole, A., 52
Midgley, M., xxxii, 131

Miller, S., 44, 125
Montouri, A., 28, 51

National Health Service (NHS), 35, 79, 83, 116, 120, 125, 131, 137–138, 142–143, 146, 148, 150

object(ive), 10, 44, 56, 100
    assessment, 132
    criteria, 112
    descriptors, 99
    formulations, 2
    inanimate, 67
    of scrutiny xx
    truth, 56
Omer, H., 122

Palmer, R. E., 5, 60, 67
Partridge, K., 100
Phillips, A., 49
prejudice, xviii, xxi, 2, 4, 26, 33, 43, 57, 67, 70, 73–74, 76, 80–81, 93, 104, 132, 157
    anti-diagnostic, 74
    contemporary, 129
    frame, xvii
    mercy of, 73
    negative, 132
    personal, 42
    presence of, 73
    sectarian, 73
    troublesome, 43
Prigogine, I., xix
Purser, R. E., 51

Ray, W. A., xviii, 4, 42, 73–74, 132, 157
resistance, xxi, 9, 24, 50, 66, 68
    non-violent (NVR), 122
Rober, P., 118
Robinson, K., 83
Royal Academy of Dramatic Art (RADA), 29
Rustin, M., 126, 149

Salamon, E., 112
Samuels, A., 108

Sandel, M., 120, 127
Schmeets, M. G. J., 90
Schon, D. A., 60
Segal, L., 37
Seikkula, J., 41, 67, 118
self, xii, xviii, 29, 57
    acquisitive, 130
    -blame, 20
    -congratulation, 39
    -corrective, 129
    -critical, 108
    -defined, 108
    -deprecating, 34
    -doubts, 19
    -importance, 53
    -oppressive, 3, 22
    –other awareness, xix, 12
    -pity, 92
    -protective, 77
    -recrimination, 24
    -refilling, 118
    -reflexivity, xviii–xix, xxii, 9, 43
    -sacrifice, 147
    social, 3
Sheen, M., 148–149
Shepherd, R., 7
Shotter, J., xxx, 99, 140–141
Simon, G., 118
Smail, D., 109, 131
Social Materialist Manifesto, 131
Stengers, I., xix
Stephens, J., 163
Stern, D. N., 41, 48, 60, 67
Stierlin, H., 84
Stratton, P., 118
Sundet, R., 118
systemic, xvi, xxii, 63, 90, 142–143, 148
    analysis, xix
    awareness, 51
    bias, 4
    conceptualisation, 131
    curiosity, xvii
    exploration, 104
    foundations, 108
    humanism, xvi, xxii, xxx–xxxi, 1–3, 5, 8, 12, 19, 21, 24, 37, 50,

58–59, 61, 74–75, 83–84, 90–91,
    98, 101, 108, 109, 112–113, 119,
    130–131, 134, 140, 143, 146, 151
humility, 43, 51, 69
ideas, xiii
influences, 132
information, 4
modes of consultation, 104
nature, 100, 116
positioning, xxii, 112
practice, xv–xvi, 1, 97
    radical, 1
practitioner, 49
principles, 112
process, 152
questions, xxiii
relational focus, 20
supervision, 100
therapy, xxxi, 12, 49, 74, 90, 153

family, xxxii, 1
way, xix
work, xx

Tallis, R., 42, 125, 139, 150
Taylor, B., 49
Taylor Robinson, H., 7

Verheugt-Pleiter, A. J. E., 90

Walrond-Skinner, S., 102
Wampold, B. E., 76, 118
Watzlawick, P., 37
Weakland, J. H., 37
White, M., 105
Wilson, J., xi–xii, xv–xxiv, 1, 7, 48, 74, 76, 87, 92

Zevalkink, J., 90

v